PROUDLY PRESENTS

# The 2008 NFL & NCAA FOOTBALL

# POWER SYSTEM

# WORKBOOK

**50** PERFECT **POWER SYSTEMS** from the **PRO INFO SPORTS**

*2008 NFL & NCAA Football POWER SYSTEM e-CYCLOPEDIAS*

# TABLE of CONTENTS

## NFL POWER SYSTEMS

## UNDERSTANDING & USING NCAA FOOTBALL POWER SYSTEMS          37

# NCAA FOOTBALL POWER SYSTEMS

# INTRODUCTION

**PRO INFO SPORTS** is dedicated to providing our clients with ideal investment opportunities and intelligent recommendations for financial success in the sports gaming global market. To that end, we have produced **NFL POWER SYSTEM e-CYCLOPEDIAS** on CD-ROM and e-BOOK for several seasons, containing our entire collection of NFL **POWER SYSTEMS** from the past 25+ seasons. It has grown and improved with each edition, and the 2008 version contains *over 800* NFL **POWER SYSTEMS!**

At the request of many college football fans, we added an **NCAA Football POWER SYSTEM e-CYCLOPEDIA** in later years. Together, these collections contain *over 1700* **POWER SYSTEMS**, all of which are 100% ATS! Every common football scenario is covered by 25 sections in each e-CYCLOPEDIA.

From those 50 combined sections, we have carefully selected a top **POWER SYSTEM** to create the *2008 NFL & NCAA FOOTBALL POWER SYSTEM WORKBOOK*. This product is designed to equip buyers with some POWERful handicapping tools for the 2008 football season, and to introduce them to what else **PRO INFO SPORTS** has to offer sports investors. Used properly with sound handicapping and money management strategies, **POWER SYSTEMS** can be part of a highly profitable game plan. We encourage you to read the entire *Introduction* to maximize their potential.

In addition to this workbook and the full NFL & NCAA Football **POWER SYSTEM** e-CYCLOPEDIAS, other **PRO INFO SPORTS** Products & Services include **POWERePORTS**, **POWERePLAYS**, and **GAMEDAY INVESTMENT e-LERTS**, which are covered last in the *Introduction*. When online, you're invited to visit us at **www.proinfosports.com**, our Internet home of professional information, analysis, and advice for sports investors.

## *Investing* or *Gambling?*

Sports gaming can be favorably compared to the stock market because few investments in stocks or bonds can offer the profit potential that professional-grade sports investing does. It is not a "get-rich-quick scheme", as financial gains can initially be modest; however, with a comprehensive strategy such as provided by **PRO INFO SPORTS** and the discipline to execute it, the profitable possibilities are quite impressive. Armed with such a game plan you could easily see a doubling of your investment in less than a year's time. What stocks offer comparable returns?

Of course there are no guarantees in the stock market or sports investing. **PRO INFO SPORTS** minimizes the risk for loss while being as aggressive in our investment strategy as is prudent in order to maximize profits; however, we strongly urge a sports investor to only assume a financial position that he or she can afford to lose. No different than the DOW or NASDAQ, profits from sports wagering can fluctuate from day to day. Painstaking research and careful planning can mean nothing in the face of a streak of simple bad luck. The gains, losses, ups and downs are simply part of the game, and have to be played out. Over an extended period of time a profit is ultimately produced. If you have a practical perspective on sports gaming and investing, you will be greatly satisfied with the monetary results you can realize with the help of **PRO INFO SPORTS** and this *2008 NFL & NCAA FOOTBALL **POWER SYSTEM** Workbook.*

Despite the upside potential, statistics indicate only 19% of self-advised bettors will turn a profit on any given weekend, and this percentage drops further throughout the course of a sports season into the single digits. This is why the comprehensive handicapping and money management strategies are crucial in providing the difference between intelligent investing and irrational gambling. Read more about sports gaming investments at:
**www.proinfosports.com/investing-or-gambling-on-sports.php**.

## *Handicapping*

**PRO INFO SPORTS** has adopted, mastered, and refined prevailing sports gaming investment techniques and combined them with our own successful methodologies, including **POWER SYSTEMS**, to achieve impressive, consistent winning results. Being a successful sports gaming investor requires time, effort, and resources. In real estate, the three most important factors are LOCATION, LOCATION, and LOCATION. In handicapping, it's INFORMATION, INFORMATION, and INFORMATION. Gathering information through TV, radio, newspapers, and the Internet is vital. Statistical information can be used to determine an initial "power ratings" for both teams in a game and compared to the posted pointspread for potential line value.

Next, each team's physical, psychological, and emotional states must be examined by a non-mathematical analysis of dynamics such as motivation, injuries, weather, distractions, and other intangible factors. The consideration of these subjective factors allows for a more precise determination of the actual strength of each team in a matchup.

Finally, an investigation of the technical circumstances of each team can often yield meaningful historical trends. How teams have performed under certain conditions in the past, such as when home/away, a favorite/underdog, in a divisional/non-divisional game, etc., can portend future outcomes. In addition to established, simple single-team and single-factor angles, **PRO INFO SPORTS** employs our own unique and complex *league-wide* systems in our handicapping arsenal. These are known as **POWER SYSTEMS.**

Some trends are absolutely meaningless. They have happened for no particular reason, so there's no particular reason for them to continue. The Dallas Cowboys had an interesting trend of losing their tenth game of the season for 10 years in a row, from 1987 through 1996. "Scamdicappers" sold that trend and continue to sell such information that has no possible reasoning. Dallas won their tenth game of the 1997 season, bringing that trend to an end. It was a simple, single-team trend that did not have a logical reason to continue. **PRO INFO SPORTS** ignores such useless "number noise".

The **POWER SYSTEMS** in this workbook are far superior, as they are league wide *and* have very sound handicapping principles behind them. Even some of these systems can become outdated, so we concentrate on those that are still producing consistent winning situations and those that are recent, but already very strong.

In the 1980s and into the 90s, Monday Night Football home underdogs were a solid play, and with good reason. The prime time lights and national attention usually brought out the best in the home teams. Additionally, even the underdogs on Monday Nights are going to most often be good teams, and such teams usually perform strongly as underdogs, any day of the week. Eventually, though, the wagering public caught on to this trend and bet accordingly. The pointspreads were adjusted and now there is little line value in blindly betting Monday Night Football home dogs. Since the start of the 2001 season, such teams are a bankroll-busting 13-24 against the spread.

The bottom line is that you should never use a trend or system without sound reasoning and a strong record of performance to back it up. With *The 2008 NFL & NCAA FOOTBALL* **POWER SYSTEM** *WORKBOOK*, you get both. Even then, you should not bet a game solely on the basis of one or more systems.

The relative importance of fundamental, situational, and technical factors, including these **POWER SYSTEMS** fluctuate from team to team and from game to game. Sports gaming expertise is established upon the intelligent and insightful consideration and application of these factors in conjunction with a sound money management strategy. More of our handicapping insights are available at: **www.proinfosports.com/handicapping-sports.php**.

### *Money Management*

Successful sports gaming has as much to do with money management as it does with sports. It is no exaggeration when **PRO INFO SPORTS** declares the following: A positive return on investment is just as dependent upon rational financial administration as it is upon handicapping acumen. In fact, the absence of sound money management or use of a flawed system can negate even a long-term advantage in any type of investing and result in a net loss.

Profitable money management via any potentially lucrative method requires discipline. It is critical to first establish available risk capital. This is the amount of money assigned for investing. It should never be from funds reserved for basic living expenses. It is money that if completely lost would not alter one's standard of living. Discipline is also required in sports gaming for investing the proper amount of each wager as determined by a sound strategy and not deviating from the game plan. For maximum financial rewards, a suitable fiscal plan must be precisely planned, followed and executed.

**PRO INFO SPORTS** has developed a powerful money management strategy, applying the superior investing principle of wagering a *percentage* of available capital rather than a constant *flat* dollar amount. What the average sports investor fails to understand is that for the greatest return on any series of wagering opportunities there is a *precise percentage of bankroll* that should be risked. Even with more winners than losers, betting considerably more or less than the "magic number" will ultimately result in a net loss. We have named this optimal figure the *Peak Profit Percentage* or, for short, **PPP**.

Having a realistic expectation in sports wagering is imperative. **PRO INFO SPORTS** is confident that we will to continue to offer our clients a winning expectation of 55%-60% for our highest-rated plays. Looking at the figures within that range, a **Peak Profit Percentage** of 5% can be calculated from the low end (55% winners) and a **PPP** of 15% at the high end (60% winners).

Taking the riskiest position with a $1000 bankroll (wagering 15% per game) would actually result in a net loss of $348 after 100 events if the winning percentage actually turned out to be at the low end of 55%. On the other hand, taking the most conservative position (5% wagers) with a $1000 bankroll will show a profit after 100 games, ranging from $148 (with 55% winners) to $944 (60% winners), so we find that there is no overall advantage of risking *more* than 5% of current bankroll on a contest. Applying the same investment principles to our remaining plays, which have a slightly lower (but still profitable) winning expectation, we have developed a system of 2-5% investments.

Those at the other extreme that contend only 1% at the most should ever be wagered on one game are also oblivious to the **Peak Profit Percentage** principle. Wagering 5% per event will only be a losing proposition if the winning percentage slides down to 53%, at which point a starting bankroll of $1000 would be trimmed by a mere $70 after 100 wagers. Placing 1% wagers with a $1000 bankroll and a 53% winning percentage would show a profit of only $8 after 100 events, while 2% wagers would return a net profit of just $4. A winning percentage of 52.5% (the break even point) or less will not show a profit regardless of how small the bankroll percent wagered is, so we find that there is no overall advantage of risking just 1% on every game. This is a small example of the comprehensive, analytical manner in which **PRO INFO SPORTS** narrowed the recommended individual investment amounts to **2-5%** of current bankroll, as calculated before each investment.

Finally, we resolved the question of how many such events would be financially prudent to wager simultaneously. It was calculated that putting to work *up to 25%* of a bankroll at one time on a consistent basis offers the greatest potential for compounding profits without being unnecessarily risky *if* enough worthy investment opportunities are available. A much more thorough and complete examination and explanation of our superior money management strategy is available online at: **www.proinfosports.com/gambling-money-management.php**.

It must always be remembered that sports gaming is to be approached on a professional level. Be mentally and emotionally prepared for the ups and downs that will occur simply due to the laws of averages and inherent with investing. Applying sound handicapping principles, including **POWER SYSTEMS** and money management skills on a consistent basis will ultimately produce outstanding returns.

### *Additional Notes*

On the **PRO INFO SPORTS** website you will find many helpful tools. Our **Injuries** and **Weather** pages provide valuable insight into these handicapping factors, including links to the latest injury and weather developments for every NFL and NCAA Football team at the following links:
**www.proinfosports.com/injury-reports.php**
**www.proinfosports.com/weather-reports.php**.

Lines and live scores are available on our **Odds & Scores** page at:
**www.proinfosports.com/sports-odds-scores.php**.

Links to various sports information websites and gaming forums can be found on the **Sports Handicapping Resources** page at:
**www.proinfosports.com/sports-handicappers-resources.php**.


## *Other Products & Services*

As a superior sports investment firm, **PRO INFO SPORTS** can charge *less* for our expertise. It is by design that our products and services are priced for a potential client to try for a week or month before making a longer commitment and for less money than a single "super-duper lock" or "1-million-star game" might cost from some "scamdicappers". These touts try take as much money as quickly as possible from the unsuspecting because they know the customers won't be back.

We, on the other hand, are certain that our sports-gaming handicapping and money management excellence will continue to turn trial customers into long-term clients, and the **PRO INFO SPORTS** Products & Services are priced with that supreme confidence in mind.

In addition to this workbook, **POWER SYSTEM** Products and Services include **NFL** and **NCAA Football POWER SYSTEM e-CYCLOPEDIAS**, along with **NFL** and **NCAA Football POWERePORTS** and **POWERePLAYS** via season, monthly, weekly, and game subscriptions.

➢ **POWER SYSTEM e-CYCLOPEDIAS** on CD-ROM and e-BOOK are the entire collections of nearly 2000 100% ATS NFL and NCAA Football **POWER SYSTEMS** from nearly 30 seasons. Every common football scenario is covered by 50 Sections. This workbook features *one* **POWER SYSTEM** from each of those sections.

➢ **POWERePORT** clients have access to ALL current, updated, and new **POWER SYSTEMS** active for each game. **POWERePORTS** are also useful for **e-CYCLOPEDIA** customers who want updates to eliminate losing parameters from current systems, to be informed of the discovery of new systems as they emerge, and to avoid searching for active systems. **NFL**, **NCAA Football**, and **Total Football POWERePORT** subscriptions are available by the Season, Month, Week, and Game.

➢ **POWERePLAY** clients have access to the TOP current, updated, or new **POWER SYSTEM** active for each game. **POWERePLAYS** are also useful for **e-CYCLOPEDIA** customers who want to avoid searching for active systems and just want the highest-graded system available for each contest. **NFL**, **NCAA Football**, and **Total Football POWERePLAY** subscriptions are available by the Season, Month, Week, and Game.

➢ **POWER FREe-PLAY** recipients enjoy FREE NFL & NCAA Football **POWER SYSTEMS** that demonstrate the POWER of the technical information offered by **PRO INFO SPORTS**. If you would like to join the FREe-PLAY e-mail list, send us your request at **win@proinfosports.com**. You can also check our FREE page for complimentary **POWER SYSTEMS** at: **www.proinfosports.com/free-sports-picks.php**.

More information on **PRO INFO SPORTS POWER SYSTEMS** can be found at: **www.proinfosports.com/sports-handicapping-systems.php**.

➢ **PRO INFO SPORTS** clients can also receive a **GAMEDAY INVESTMENT e-LERT** the day *of* all basketball (NBA and NCAA) and Major League Baseball games and the day *prior* to all football games (NFL and NCAA), detailing each **Money Play** and **Opinion Selection** with comprehensive information, analysis and advice. There are season, monthly, weekly, and game subscriptions available for NFL and NCAA Football **E-LERTS.**

➢ A **GAMEDAY INVESTMENT FREe-LERT** is also available, featuring a sample of the in-depth information, analysis, and advice offered from **PRO INFO SPORTS.** View these frequent complimentary selections at **www.proinfosports.com/free-sports-picks.php**. If you would like to receive the **FREe-LERT** via e-mail, simply send a request to **WIN@proinfosports.com**.

Complete examples of **GAMEDAY INVESTMENT e-LERTS** along with details and pricing information on all **PRO INFO SPORTS** Products & Service can be found at: **www.proinfosports.com/sports-picks.php**.

For complete details and pricing information on all **PRO INFO SPORTS** Products & Services, visit **www.proinfosports.com/sports-picks.php**.

## UNDERSTANDING & USING NFL POWER SYSTEMS

There is a wealth of information contained within the explanation, parameters, and results of each **POWER SYSTEM.** It is vital to be familiar with all of these features to get the maximum benefit from this workbook. Every computer-researched **PRO INFO SPORTS POWER SYSTEM** is documented with:

> **Brief explanation** of the situation and why it holds value.

> **Parameters** revealing the precise circumstances in which the system will be active.

> **SU record** & **SU margin** summarizing the Straight Up record and average outright winning margin of the system.

> **ATS record** & **ATS margin** summarizing the Against The Spread record and average winning spread margin of the system.

> **Chart** listing the historical information of all qualifying games with columns for:

   o YEAR
   o WEEK
   o DAY
   o TEAM
   o OPPONENT
   o SITE
   o LINE
   o SCORE
   o SU RESULT & MARGIN
   o ATS RESULT & MARGIN in **BOLD**
   o 2007 results in *italics*
   o Blank Lines for writing in 2008 qualifying games and results

## NFL POWER SYSTEM Notes:

➢ Many systems contain the word "vs." which refers to the system team's *current* opponent and not a previous one.

➢ A slash ("/") means *or.* A "SU win/SU tie" refers to a SU win *or* SU tie.

➢ A team's "last game" may have come before a bye week if they are rested; however, if a system refers to "last week", teams off a bye would *not* qualify. The same principles apply to the terms "next game" and "next week".

➢ "Game number" refers to a *team's* game number, while "Week number" refers to the *league's* week number. These numbers will be the same for a team until it has a bye, at which point its "game number" will be one less than the league "week number".

➢ Figures like "sub-.870%", ".750%+", "+.250%", etc. refer to *winning percentage*.

➢ NFL team abbreviations used will be obvious to football fans; however, several teams have moved in the 25+ seasons covered by our systems. Each team is identified by its *current* city abbreviation, regardless of where they may have been located previously. "IND" refers to all Colts games, whether in Indianapolis or Baltimore. "BAL" refers to the Baltimore Ravens and previous Cleveland Browns teams, while "CLE" refers only to the expansion Cleveland Browns. "HOU" is used for the Houston Texans only, while "TEN" is used for the Tennessee Titans and Houston Oilers teams. "ARZ" refers to all Cardinals games, whether playing out of Arizona, Phoenix, or St. Louis, and "STL" is used for all Rams games, whether playing out of St. Louis or Los Angeles. Finally, "OAK" refers to all Raiders games, whether in Oakland or Los Angeles.

➢ 1987 "strike" games played by replacement players were not used in the systems.

Send your **POWER SYSTEM** questions and comments to **WIN@ProInfoSports.com**.

For those interested in verifying our **POWER SYSTEMS** and/or researching their own systems, **PRO INFO SPORTS** recommends the user-friendly databases at www.KillerSports.com and www.Sportsdatabase.com.

# NFL POWER SYSTEM #1

*Section 1* of the **PRO INFO SPORTS 2008 NFL POWER SYSTEM e-CYCLOPEDIA** deals exclusively with early-season situations in the NFL. The system below has been perfect for 2 decades, beating the spread by more than 10 points a game on average.

After starting the season with a big win over a division foe, underdogs have been unable to come up with another solid performance in their next game.

In **Game 2,** play **AGAINST** a non-Monday underdog/pick 'em off a division SU win of 7+ points in its last game and *not* before a bye next week.

SU: 19-0 (13.9)    **ATS: 18-0-1 (10.2)**

| YEAR | WK | DAY | TEAM | OPP | ST | LINE | SCORE | SU | MRG | ATS | MRG |
|------|----|-----|------|-----|----|------|-------|----|----|-----|-----|
| 1988 | 2 | SUN | NE | MIN | A | +6' | 6-36 | L | -30 | L | -23' |
| 1988 | 2 | SUN | OAK | TEN | A | +2' | 35-38 | L | -3 | L | -0' |
| 1989 | 2 | SUN | OAK | KC | A | +2' | 19-24 | L | -5 | L | -2' |
| 1990 | 2 | SUN | WAS | SF | A | +4' | 13-26 | L | -13 | L | -8' |
| 1990 | 2 | SUN | TB | STL | H | +3 | 14-35 | L | -21 | L | -18 |
| 1991 | 2 | SUN | NE | CLE | H | 0 | 0-20 | L | -20 | L | -20 |
| 1995 | 2 | SUN | TEN | PIT | H | +4' | 17-34 | L | -17 | L | -12' |
| 1995 | 2 | SUN | WAS | OAK | H | +4' | 8-20 | L | -12 | L | -7' |
| 1997 | 2 | SUN | NYG | JAC | A | +3' | 13-40 | L | -27 | L | -23' |
| 1998 | 2 | SUN | DAL | DEN | A | +7 | 23-42 | L | -19 | L | -12 |
| 1998 | 2 | SUN | KC | JAC | A | +4' | 16-21 | L | -5 | L | -0' |
| 1998 | 2 | SUN | NYG | OAK | A | +2 | 17-20 | L | -3 | L | -1 |
| 1999 | 2 | SUN | IND | NE | A | +3 | 28-31 | L | -3 | P | 0 |
| 2000 | 2 | SUN | JAC | BAL | A | +2' | 36-39 | L | -3 | L | -0' |
| 2000 | 2 | SUN | ATL | DEN | A | +4 | 14-42 | L | -28 | L | -24 |
| 2003 | 2 | SUN | PIT | KC | A | +3' | 20-41 | L | -21 | L | -17' |
| 2004 | 2 | SUN | STL | ATL | A | +2 | 17-34 | L | -17 | L | -15 |
| 2004 | 2 | SUN | CLE | DAL | A | +5 | 12-19 | L | -7 | L | -2 |
| 2006 | 2 | SUN | ARZ | SEA | A | +7 | 10-21 | L | -11 | L | -4 |
| ____ | _ | ___ | ____ | ____ | _ | ___ | ____ | _ | __ | _ | __ |
| ____ | _ | ___ | ____ | ____ | _ | ___ | ____ | _ | __ | _ | __ |
| ____ | _ | ___ | ____ | ____ | _ | ___ | ____ | _ | __ | _ | __ |

# NFL POWER SYSTEM #2

This **POWER SYSTEM** from *Section 2* of the **PRO INFO SPORTS 2008 NFL e-CYCLOPEDIA** is one of our top mid-season scenarios. The situation described has been going strong since at least the early 1980s and produced 2 more winners last season.

After starting the season poorly at 1-3, teams at the right price have been very strong getting back on track against division opponents.

In **Game 5,** play **ON** a .250% non-Monday division team (*not* a favorite of 7+ points *or* underdog of more than 9 points) vs. an opponent off a SU win in its last game.

SU: 16-3-1 (8.2)     **ATS: 20-0 (9.1)**

| YEAR | WK | DAY | TEAM | OPP | ST | LINE | SCORE | SU | MRG | ATS | MRG |
|------|----|-----|------|-----|----|------|-------|----|----|-----|-----|
| 1981 | 5 | SUN | ARZ | DAL | H | +6 | 20-17 | W | 3 | W | +9 |
| 1981 | 5 | SUN | CHI | MIN | A | +5 | 21-24 | L | -3 | W | +2 |
| 1981 | 5 | SUN | NYJ | MIA | A | +6 | 28-28 | T | 0 | W | +6 |
| 1982 | 5 | THU | SF | STL | A | -3 | 30-24 | W | 6 | W | +3 |
| 1985 | 5 | SUN | GB | DET | H | -3' | 43-10 | W | 33 | W | +29' |
| 1986 | 5 | SUN | OAK | KC | A | -1 | 24-17 | W | 7 | W | +6 |
| 1988 | 5 | SUN | DEN | SD | A | -4 | 12-0 | W | 12 | W | +8 |
| 1988 | 5 | SUN | NE | IND | H | -2' | 21-17 | W | 4 | W | +1' |
| 1989 | 5 | SUN | KC | SEA | A | +7' | 20-16 | W | 4 | W | +11' |
| 1990 | 6 | SUN | ARZ | DAL | H | -1 | 20-3 | W | 17 | W | +16 |
| 1991 | 5 | SUN | NYJ | MIA | H | +1' | 41-23 | W | 18 | W | +19' |
| 1997 | 6 | SUN | PHI | WAS | H | -3 | 24-10 | W | 14 | W | +11 |
| 1998 | 6 | SUN | TEN | BAL | A | +3 | 12-8 | W | 4 | W | +7 |
| 1998 | 6 | SUN | CIN | PIT | H | +2' | 25-20 | W | 5 | W | +7' |
| 1998 | 6 | SUN | BUF | IND | A | -2' | 31-24 | W | 7 | W | +4' |
| 1999 | 5 | SUN | ARZ | NYG | H | -2 | 14-3 | W | 11 | W | +9 |
| 2001 | 6 | SUN | CAR | NO | H | +4' | 25-27 | L | -2 | W | +2' |
| 2003 | 5 | SUN | NO | CAR | A | +7 | 13-19 | L | -6 | W | +1 |
| 2005 | 5 | SUN | BUF | MIA | H | -3 | 20-14 | W | 6 | W | +3 |
| 2005 | 6 | SUN | BAL | CLE | H | -6 | 16-3 | W | 13 | W | +7 |
| *2007* | *5* | *SUN* | *CHI* | *GB* | *A* | *+3'* | *27-20* | *W* | *7* | *W* | *+10'* |
| *2007* | *6* | *SUN* | *MIN* | *CHI* | *A* | *+5'* | *34-31* | *W* | *3* | *W* | *+8'* |
| ___ | _ | ___ | ___ | ___ | _ | ___ | ___ | _ | ___ | _ | ___ |
| ___ | _ | ___ | ___ | ___ | _ | ___ | ___ | _ | ___ | _ | ___ |
| ___ | _ | ___ | ___ | ___ | _ | ___ | ___ | _ | ___ | _ | ___ |

# NFL POWER SYSTEM #3

*Section 3* of the **PRO INFO SPORTS 2008 NFL POWER SYSTEM e-CYCLOPEDIA** examines many late-season situations. The featured scenario below has very basic parameters, but qualifying teams have gone an amazing 26 games without a spread win.

After 11 or more games, division home favorites have been very weak when coming off a home SU loss and a road game prior to that.

From **Game 12 on,** play **AGAINST** a division home favorite off a home SU loss of less than 26 points last week and a road contest in its game before that.

SU: 19-7 (4.8)          **ATS: 25-0-1 (10.6)**

| YEAR | WK | DAY | TEAM | OPP | ST | LINE | SCORE | SU | MRG | ATS | MRG |
|------|----|-----|------|-----|----|------|-------|----|----|-----|-----|
| 1993 | 14 | MON | DAL | PHI | H | -16' | 23-17 | W | 6 | L | -10' |
| 1993 | 14 | SUN | DET | MIN | H | -3 | 0-13 | L | -13 | L | -16 |
| 1993 | 17 | SUN | CHI | DET | H | -3 | 14-20 | L | -6 | L | -9 |
| 1994 | 13 | SUN | MIN | TB | H | -14 | 17-20 | L | -3 | L | -17 |
| 1994 | 16 | SUN | BUF | NE | H | -1' | 17-41 | L | -24 | L | -25' |
| 1995 | 15 | SUN | NE | NYJ | H | -7 | 31-28 | W | 3 | L | -4 |
| 1995 | 17 | SAT | IND | NE | H | -5' | 10-7 | W | 3 | L | -2' |
| 1996 | 15 | SUN | DET | MIN | H | -2 | 22-24 | L | -2 | L | -4 |
| 1996 | 15 | SUN | NO | ATL | H | -2 | 15-31 | L | -16 | L | -18 |
| 1996 | 16 | SUN | TEN | CIN | H | -4 | 13-21 | L | -8 | L | -12 |
| 1997 | 15 | SUN | ARZ | WAS | H | -1 | 28-38 | L | -10 | L | -11 |
| 1997 | 17 | SAT | CAR | STL | H | -5 | 18-30 | L | -12 | L | -17 |
| 2000 | 13 | SUN | STL | NO | H | -13' | 24-31 | L | -7 | L | -20' |
| 2000 | 14 | SUN | WAS | NYG | H | -6 | 7-9 | L | -2 | L | -8 |
| 2000 | 16 | SUN | MIA | IND | H | -3 | 13-20 | L | -7 | L | -10 |
| 2001 | 14 | SUN | CIN | JAC | H | -1 | 10-14 | L | -4 | L | -5 |
| 2001 | 14 | SUN | OAK | KC | H | -9 | 28-26 | W | 2 | L | -7 |
| 2001 | 18 | SUN | TEN | CIN | H | -5' | 21-23 | L | -2 | L | -7' |
| 2002 | 13 | SUN | SF | SEA | H | -9' | 31-24 | W | 7 | L | -2' |
| 2002 | 17 | SUN | IND | JAC | H | -8 | 20-13 | W | 7 | L | -1 |
| 2003 | 14 | SUN | NYG | WAS | H | -3 | 7-20 | L | -13 | L | -16 |
| 2004 | 16 | SUN | DET | CHI | H | -6 | 19-13 | W | 6 | P | 0 |
| 2004 | 16 | SUN | TB | CAR | H | -3 | 20-37 | L | -17 | L | -20 |
| 2005 | 16 | SAT | STL | SF | H | -9 | 20-24 | L | -4 | L | -13 |
| 2006 | 16 | SUN | ATL | CAR | H | -6' | 3-10 | L | -7 | L | -13' |
| *2007* | *14* | *SUN* | *PHI* | *NYG* | *H* | *-3* | *13-16* | *L* | *-3* | *L* | *-6* |
| —— | — | —— | ——— | ——— | — | —— | ——— | — | —— | — | —— |
| —— | — | —— | ——— | ——— | — | —— | ——— | — | —— | — | —— |
| —— | — | —— | ——— | ——— | — | —— | ——— | — | —— | — | —— |

# NFL POWER SYSTEM #4

We have discovered many strong situations that apply exclusively to the final game of the NFL regular season and feature these **POWER SYSTEMS** in *Section 4* of the **PRO INFO SPORTS 2008 NFL e-CYCLOPEDIA**. The following system enjoyed 2 more paydays last season, and has been perfect for over 20 years.

Division home teams at the right price have finished the season in very strong fashion against teams with solid winning records.

In **Game 16,** play **ON** a division home team (*not* a favorite of 10+ points *or* underdog of more than 2 points) vs. a +.600% opponent.

SU: 15-0 (12.6)     **ATS: 15-0 (10.6)**

| YEAR | WK | DAY | TEAM | OPP | ST | LINE | SCORE | SU | MRG | ATS | MRG |
|------|----|-----|------|-----|----|------|-------|----|----|-----|-----|
| 1986 | 16 | SUN | SEA | DEN | H | -3' | 41-16 | W | 25 | **W** | **+21'** |
| 1988 | 16 | SUN | IND | BUF | H | +2 | 17-14 | W | 3 | **W** | **+5** |
| 1988 | 16 | SUN | BAL | TEN | H | -2' | 28-23 | W | 5 | **W** | **+2'** |
| 1989 | 16 | SUN | SD | DEN | H | +1' | 16-10 | W | 6 | **W** | **+7'** |
| 1994 | 17 | SAT | NYG | DAL | H | +2 | 15-10 | W | 5 | **W** | **+7** |
| 1996 | 17 | SUN | SD | DEN | H | +1' | 16-10 | W | 6 | **W** | **+7'** |
| 1996 | 17 | SUN | WAS | DAL | H | -3' | 37-10 | W | 27 | **W** | **+23'** |
| 1997 | 17 | SUN | TEN | PIT | H | -3 | 16-6 | W | 10 | **W** | **+7** |
| 1999 | 17 | SUN | BUF | IND | H | +2 | 31-6 | W | 25 | **W** | **+27** |
| 2000 | 17 | SUN | GB | TB | H | -2 | 17-14 | W | 3 | **W** | **+1** |
| 2002 | 17 | SAT | NYG | PHI | H | -1 | 10-7 | W | 3 | **W** | **+2** |
| 2002 | 17 | MON | STL | SF | H | -2 | 31-20 | W | 11 | **W** | **+9** |
| 2005 | 17 | SUN | MIN | CHI | H | -4' | 34-10 | W | 24 | **W** | **+19'** |
| *2007* | *17* | *SUN* | *WAS* | *DAL* | *H* | *-9* | *27-6* | *W* | *21* | ***W*** | ***+12*** |
| *2007* | *17* | *SUN* | *HOU* | *JAC* | *H* | *-7* | *42-28* | *W* | *14* | ***W*** | ***+7*** |

# NFL POWER SYSTEM #5

In *Section 5* of the **PRO INFO SPORTS 2008 NFL POWER SYSTEM e-CYCLOPEDIA** we feature teams enjoying perfect seasons and teams suffering a winless start. The selected situation described below has been a winner since at least the early 1980s.

After dropping to 0-4, but allowing 33 points or less, home favorites and small underdogs have been quite formidable.

In **Game 5,** play **ON** a winless non-Monday home team (*not* an underdog of 6+ points) off allowing less than 34 points in its last game.

SU: 12-3 (9.0)          **ATS: 15-0 (8.2)**

| YEAR | WK | DAY | TEAM | OPP | ST | LINE | SCORE | SU | MRG | ATS | MRG |
|------|----|-----|------|-----|----|------|-------|----|-----|-----|-----|
| 1981 | 5 | SUN | NE | KC | H | -5' | 33-17 | W | 16 | **W** | **+10'** |
| 1991 | 5 | SUN | SD | KC | H | +3' | 13-14 | L | -1 | **W** | **+2'** |
| 1992 | 5 | SUN | NYJ | NE | H | -8' | 30-21 | W | 9 | **W** | **+0'** |
| 1992 | 5 | SUN | OAK | NYG | H | +2 | 13-10 | W | 3 | **W** | **+5** |
| 1992 | 5 | SUN | SD | SEA | H | -4 | 17-6 | W | 11 | **W** | **+7** |
| 1998 | 5 | SUN | CHI | DET | H | -2 | 31-27 | W | 4 | **W** | **+2** |
| 1998 | 5 | SUN | IND | SD | H | -1 | 17-12 | W | 5 | **W** | **+4** |
| 1999 | 5 | SUN | CLE | CIN | H | +3 | 17-18 | L | -1 | **W** | **+2** |
| 2001 | 7 | SUN | DET | TEN | H | +5 | 24-27 | L | -3 | **W** | **+2** |
| 2003 | 5 | SUN | JAC | SD | H | -3 | 27-21 | W | 6 | **W** | **+3** |
| 2003 | 6 | SUN | NYJ | BUF | H | +1' | 30-3 | W | 27 | **W** | **+28'** |
| 2004 | 5 | SUN | SF | ARZ | H | -1 | 31-28 | W | 3 | **W** | **+2** |
| 2004 | 6 | SUN | BUF | MIA | H | -5 | 20-13 | W | 7 | **W** | **+2** |
| 2005 | 5 | SUN | GB | NO | H | -3 | 52-3 | W | 49 | **W** | **+46** |
| 2006 | 6 | SUN | TB | CIN | H | +4 | 14-13 | W | 1 | **W** | **+5** |
| —— | — | —— | —— | —— | — | —— | —— | — | — | — | —— |
| —— | — | —— | —— | —— | — | —— | —— | — | — | — | —— |
| —— | — | —— | —— | —— | — | —— | —— | — | — | — | —— |

# NFL POWER SYSTEM #6

We take a look at favorites, whether at home or on the road in *Section 6* of the **PRO INFO SPORTS 2008 NFL POWER SYSTEM e-CYCLOPEDIA.** The system below has been going strong since 1989 and after taking last year off is due to come up this season.

After running wild in a victory over a division rival, single-digit favorites have had a very hard time continuing the momentum under the conditions outlined.

Play **AGAINST** a favorite of less than 10 points off a division SU win, rushing for 250+ yards last week vs. an opponent *not* off a home division SU loss in its last game.

SU: 12-9 (4.1)        **ATS: 21-0 (9.4)**

| YEAR | WK | DAY | TEAM | OPP | ST | LINE | SCORE | SU | MRG | ATS | MRG |
|------|----|-----|------|-----|----|------|-------|----|-----|-----|-----|
| 1989 | 9  | SUN | BUF  | ATL | A  | -3'  | 28-30 | L  | -2  | L   | -5' |
| 1990 | 4  | SUN | BUF  | DEN | H  | -4   | 29-28 | W  | 1   | L   | -3  |
| 1991 | 13 | SUN | BUF  | NE  | A  | -8   | 13-16 | L  | -3  | L   | -11 |
| 1991 | 16 | SUN | MIN  | STL | H  | -9   | 20-14 | W  | 6   | L   | -3  |
| 1992 | 7  | SUN | NYG  | STL | A  | -1'  | 17-38 | L  | -21 | L   | -22'|
| 1993 | 16 | SUN | STL  | CIN | A  | -2   | 3-15  | L  | -12 | L   | -14 |
| 1994 | 16 | SUN | GB   | ATL | H  | -8'  | 21-17 | W  | 4   | L   | -4' |
| 1997 | 8  | SUN | DET  | NYG | H  | -6'  | 20-26 | L  | -6  | L   | -12'|
| 2000 | 2  | SUN | PHI  | NYG | H  | -3   | 18-33 | L  | -15 | L   | -18 |
| 2000 | 17 | SUN | KC   | ATL | A  | -4'  | 13-29 | L  | -16 | L   | -20'|
| 2001 | 11 | SUN | SEA  | BUF | A  | -3'  | 23-20 | W  | 3   | L   | -0' |
| 2001 | 11 | SUN | STL  | NE  | A  | -8   | 24-17 | W  | 7   | L   | -1  |
| 2002 | 9  | SUN | ATL  | BAL | H  | -7'  | 20-17 | W  | 3   | L   | -4' |
| 2002 | 9  | SUN | PHI  | CHI | A  | -7   | 19-13 | W  | 6   | L   | -1  |
| 2003 | 10 | MON | GB   | PHI | H  | -4'  | 14-17 | L  | -3  | L   | -7' |
| 2003 | 17 | SUN | BAL  | PIT | H  | -7'  | 13-10 | W  | 3   | L   | -4' |
| 2004 | 7  | MON | DEN  | CIN | A  | -6'  | 10-23 | L  | -13 | L   | -19'|
| 2004 | 9  | SUN | NYJ  | BUF | A  | -3   | 17-22 | L  | -5  | L   | -8  |
| 2006 | 3  | MON | ATL  | NO  | A  | -4   | 3-23  | L  | -20 | L   | -24 |
| 2006 | 15 | SUN | JAC  | TEN | A  | -3'  | 17-24 | L  | -7  | L   | -10'|
| 2006 | 16 | SUN | SD   | SEA | A  | -4   | 20-17 | W  | 3   | L   | -1  |
| ____ | __ | ___ | ____ | ___ | __ | ____ | _____ | __ | ___ | _ | ____ |
| ____ | __ | ___ | ____ | ___ | __ | ____ | _____ | __ | ___ | _ | ____ |
| ____ | __ | ___ | ____ | ___ | __ | ____ | _____ | __ | ___ | _ | ____ |

# NFL POWER SYSTEM #7

Just as the **PRO INFO SPORTS 2008 NFL POWER SYSTEM e-CYCLOPEDIA** features a section on favorites, *Section 7* deals exclusively with underdogs. The parameters of this situation are quite simple but the system has been rock solid since the late 1980s, including last year when it cashed 2 more times.

After being thoroughly embarrassed in the first half of a loss, teams have been greatly under-valued as an underdog.

Play **ON** an underdog off a SU loss allowing 32+ points and trailing by 29+ points at the half.

SU: 12-8 (1.8)      **ATS: 20-0 (8.8)**

| YEAR | WK | DAY | TEAM | OPP | ST | LINE | SCORE | SU | MRG | ATS | MRG |
|------|----|-----|------|-----|----|------|-------|----|-----|-----|-----|
| 1989 | 13 | MON | SEA | BUF | H | +5' | 17-16 | W | 1 | **W** | **+6'** |
| 1990 | 17 | SUN | CLE | CIN | A | +16' | 14-21 | L | -7 | **W** | **+9'** |
| 1991 | 8 | SUN | DEN | KC | H | +1' | 19-16 | W | 3 | **W** | **+4'** |
| 1991 | 13 | SUN | TB | NYG | H | +9 | 14-21 | L | -7 | **W** | **+2** |
| 1993 | 6 | SUN | NE | ARZ | A | +11 | 23-21 | W | 2 | **W** | **+13** |
| 1994 | 2 | SUN | TEN | DAL | A | +15 | 17-20 | L | -3 | **W** | **+12** |
| 1994 | 6 | SUN | WAS | PHI | A | +13 | 17-21 | L | -4 | **W** | **+9** |
| 1997 | 2 | SUN | SD | NO | A | +2' | 20-6 | W | 14 | **W** | **+16'** |
| 1998 | 6 | SUN | PHI | WAS | H | +2' | 17-12 | W | 5 | **W** | **+7'** |
| 1998 | 10 | SUN | BAL | OAK | H | +1' | 13-10 | W | 3 | **W** | **+4'** |
| 1999 | 9 | SUN | CHI | GB | A | +9 | 14-13 | W | 1 | **W** | **+10** |
| 2003 | 15 | SUN | ARZ | CAR | H | +6' | 17-20 | L | -3 | **W** | **+3'** |
| 2004 | 8 | SUN | ATL | DEN | A | +6' | 41-28 | W | 13 | **W** | **+19'** |
| 2005 | 6 | SUN | NO | ATL | H | +5' | 31-34 | L | -3 | **W** | **+2'** |
| 2005 | 14 | SUN | PHI | NYG | H | +8' | 23-26 | L | -3 | **W** | **+5'** |
| 2006 | 7 | SUN | KC | SD | H | +5' | 30-27 | W | 3 | **W** | **+8'** |
| 2006 | 9 | SUN | SF | MIN | H | +4 | 9-3 | W | 6 | **W** | **+10** |
| 2006 | 14 | SUN | GB | SF | A | +4 | 30-19 | W | 11 | **W** | **+15** |
| *2007* | *8* | *SUN* | *MIA* | *NYG* | *H* | *+9'* | *10-13* | *L* | *-3* | ***W*** | ***+6'*** |
| *2007* | *9* | *SUN* | *HOU* | *OAK* | *A* | *+3* | *24-17* | *W* | *7* | ***W*** | ***+10*** |
| ___ | _ | ___ | ___ | ___ | _ | ___ | ___ | _ | __ | _ | ___ |
| ___ | _ | ___ | ___ | ___ | _ | ___ | ___ | _ | __ | _ | ___ |
| ___ | _ | ___ | ___ | ___ | _ | ___ | ___ | _ | __ | _ | ___ |

# NFL POWER SYSTEM #8

*Section 8* of the **PRO INFO SPORTS 2008 NFL POWER SYSTEM e-CYCLOPEDIA** investigates how teams do at *home* under various conditions. The system featured here has been perfect for 10 seasons, while crushing the spread by more than 11 ppg on average.

After a shocking win as a double-digit underdog, teams have suffered let downs and been over-valued at home by the betting public.

Play **AGAINST** a non-Saturday home team off a conference SU win as an underdog of 10+ points in its last game.

SU: 15-2 (10.9)        **ATS: 17-0 (11.4)**

| YEAR | WK | DAY | TEAM | OPP | ST | LINE | SCORE | SU | MRG | ATS | MRG |
|------|----|----|------|-----|----|----|-------|----|----|-----|----|
| 1998 | 17 | SUN | CIN | TB | H | +6 | 0-35 | L | -35 | L | **-29** |
| 1999 | 6 | SUN | CHI | PHI | H | -6 | 16-20 | L | -4 | L | **-10** |
| 1999 | 11 | SUN | CLE | CAR | H | +6 | 17-31 | L | -14 | L | **-8** |
| 2000 | 4 | SUN | DAL | SF | H | -6' | 24-41 | L | -17 | L | **-23'** |
| 2000 | 11 | SUN | CAR | NO | H | 0 | 10-20 | L | -10 | L | **-10** |
| 2000 | 14 | SUN | NO | DEN | H | -1 | 23-38 | L | -15 | L | **-16** |
| 2001 | 9 | SUN | NO | NYJ | H | -6' | 9-16 | L | -7 | L | **-13'** |
| 2002 | 3 | SUN | NYG | SEA | H | -6 | 9-6 | W | 3 | L | **-3** |
| 2002 | 5 | SUN | DAL | NYG | H | 0 | 17-21 | L | -4 | L | **-4** |
| 2002 | 9 | SUN | HOU | CIN | H | -3 | 3-38 | L | -35 | L | **-38** |
| 2002 | 15 | SUN | HOU | BAL | H | +3 | 19-23 | L | -4 | L | **-1** |
| 2004 | 13 | SUN | OAK | KC | H | -1 | 27-34 | L | -7 | L | **-8** |
| 2005 | 9 | SUN | SF | NYG | H | +10' | 6-24 | L | -18 | L | **-7'** |
| 2005 | 15 | SUN | MIA | NYJ | H | -8 | 24-20 | W | 4 | L | **-4** |
| 2006 | 11 | SUN | NYJ | CHI | H | +6 | 0-10 | L | -10 | L | **-4** |
| 2006 | 11 | SUN | HOU | BUF | H | -2' | 21-24 | L | -3 | L | **-5'** |
| —— | — | —— | —— | —— | — | —— | —— | — | —— | — | —— |
| —— | — | —— | —— | —— | — | —— | —— | — | —— | — | —— |
| —— | — | —— | —— | —— | — | —— | —— | — | —— | — | —— |

# NFL POWER SYSTEM #9

In *Section 9* of the **PRO INFO SPORTS 2008 NFL POWER SYSTEM e-CYCLOPEDIA,** we isolate home favorites in various situations. Here, we reveal one that has developed quite recently, but is already a perfect 15-0 SU & ATS since 2001, annihilating the spread by nearly 2 TDs per contest.

After a loss in which they blew a TD+ lead following 1 quarter, home teams favored by 6+ points have taken out their frustrations on the visitors.

Play **ON** a home favorite of 6+ points off a favorite SU loss, leading by 7+ points after 1 quarter in its last game.

SU: 15-0 (21.9)      **ATS: 15-0 (13.0)**

| YEAR | WK | DAY | TEAM | OPP | ST | LINE | SCORE | SU | MRG | ATS | MRG |
|------|----|-----|------|-----|----|------|-------|----|-----|-----|-----|
| 2001 | 5  | SUN | DEN  | KC  | H  | -10  | 20-6  | W  | 14  | W   | +4  |
| 2001 | 10 | SUN | STL  | CAR | H  | -19' | 48-14 | W  | 34  | W   | +14' |
| 2001 | 16 | SUN | GB   | CLE | H  | -8   | 30-7  | W  | 23  | W   | +15 |
| 2001 | 18 | SUN | PIT  | CLE | H  | -6   | 28-7  | W  | 21  | W   | +15 |
| 2002 | 13 | SUN | KC   | ARZ | H  | -9'  | 49-0  | W  | 49  | W   | +39' |
| 2002 | 14 | MON | MIA  | CHI | H  | -10  | 27-9  | W  | 18  | W   | +8  |
| 2002 | 16 | SUN | ATL  | DET | H  | -11  | 36-15 | W  | 21  | W   | +10 |
| 2003 | 11 | SUN | SEA  | DET | H  | -10' | 35-14 | W  | 21  | W   | +10' |
| 2003 | 15 | SUN | NO   | NYG | H  | -7   | 45-7  | W  | 38  | W   | +31 |
| 2004 | 9  | SUN | DEN  | HOU | H  | -7   | 31-13 | W  | 18  | W   | +11 |
| 2005 | 6  | SUN | KC   | WAS | H  | -6   | 28-21 | W  | 7   | W   | +1  |
| 2005 | 14 | SUN | PIT  | CHI | H  | -6   | 21-9  | W  | 12  | W   | +6  |
| 2006 | 2  | SUN | DAL  | WAS | H  | -6'  | 27-10 | W  | 17  | W   | +10' |
| 2006 | 10 | MON | CAR  | TB  | H  | -10  | 24-10 | W  | 14  | W   | +4  |
| *2007* | *5* | *SUN* | *PIT* | *SEA* | *H* | *-6* | *21-0* | *W* | *21* | *W* | *+15* |
| ___ | _ | ___ | ___ | ___ | _ | ___ | ___ | _ | ___ | _ | ___ |
| ___ | _ | ___ | ___ | ___ | _ | ___ | ___ | _ | ___ | _ | ___ |
| ___ | _ | ___ | ___ | ___ | _ | ___ | ___ | _ | ___ | _ | ___ |

# NFL POWER SYSTEM #10

Home underdogs have proven to be a good play under many conditions; however, we feature one here that goes the other way. This **POWER SYSTEM** from *Section 10* of the **PRO INFO SPORTS 2008 NFL e-CYCLOPEDIA** details a situation in which home dogs have been teams to fade for over 2 decades, while failing to cover the spread by 2 TDs per game on average.

Underdogs at a certain price coming off 2 road losses have not been able to get turned around against a division opponent off a loss.

Play **AGAINST** a division home underdog of 3½-7 points off 2 road SU losses in its last 2 games vs. an opponent off a SU loss in its last game.

SU: 14-0 (18.3)      **ATS: 14-0 (13.7)**

| YEAR | WK | DAY | TEAM | OPP | ST | LINE | SCORE | SU | MRG | ATS | MRG |
|------|----|-----|------|-----|----|------|-------|-----|-----|-----|-----|
| 1986 | 4 | SUN | ARZ | DAL | H | +7 | 7-31 | L | -24 | L | -17 |
| 1986 | 15 | SUN | TB | GB | H | +4 | 7-21 | L | -14 | L | -10 |
| 1988 | 8 | SUN | TB | MIN | H | +3' | 20-49 | L | -29 | L | -25' |
| 1989 | 3 | SUN | DAL | WAS | H | +6 | 7-30 | L | -23 | L | -17 |
| 1991 | 10 | SUN | STL | NO | H | +4 | 17-24 | L | -7 | L | -3 |
| 1998 | 9 | SUN | BAL | JAC | H | +3' | 19-45 | L | -26 | L | -22' |
| 1998 | 13 | SUN | CHI | TB | H | +3' | 17-31 | L | -14 | L | -10' |
| 2000 | 9 | SUN | SF | STL | H | +7 | 24-34 | L | -10 | L | -3 |
| 2000 | 13 | SUN | CIN | PIT | H | +4 | 28-48 | L | -20 | L | -16 |
| 2000 | 13 | SUN | ARZ | NYG | H | +6 | 7-31 | L | -24 | L | -18 |
| 2003 | 4 | MON | CHI | GB | H | +4 | 23-38 | L | -15 | L | -11 |
| 2004 | 4 | SUN | SF | STL | H | +3' | 14-24 | L | -10 | L | -6' |
| 2005 | 17 | SUN | ATL | CAR | H | +4 | 11-44 | L | -33 | L | -29 |
| *2007* | *3* | *SUN* | *ATL* | *CAR* | *H* | *+4* | *20-27* | *L* | *-7* | *L* | *-3* |
| ___ | _ | ___ | ___ | ___ | _ | ___ | ___ | _ | ___ | _ | ___ |
| ___ | _ | ___ | ___ | ___ | _ | ___ | ___ | _ | ___ | _ | ___ |

# NFL POWER SYSTEM #11

*Section 11* of the **PRO INFO SPORTS 2008 NFL POWER SYSTEM e-CYCLOPEDIA** looks at many situations involving teams on the road. While many bettors are hesitant to back a visiting team, this featured system is simple but has been phenomenally strong and consistent, going 18-0 ATS since at least the early 1980s, while demolishing the spread by more than 2 TDs per game on average.

After blowing a game as a big road favorite, teams back on the road have responded very strongly when playing back-to-back division opponents.

Play **ON** a non-Monday road team off a SU loss/tie as a road favorite of 7+ points in its last game and *not* playing its 2nd straight division opponent.

SU: 16-2 (15.7)     **ATS: 18-0 (14.4)**

| YEAR | WK | DAY | TEAM | OPP | ST | LINE | SCORE | SU | MRG | ATS | MRG |
|------|----|-----|------|-----|----|----|-------|----|-----|-----|-----|
| 1982 | 8 | SUN | GB | ATL | A | +4 | 38-7 | W | 31 | **W** | **+35** |
| 1985 | 8 | SUN | SF | ARZ | A | -1 | 28-14 | W | 14 | **W** | **+13** |
| 1988 | 12 | SUN | CIN | DAL | A | -5' | 38-24 | W | 14 | **W** | **+8'** |
| 1991 | 9 | SUN | MIN | ARZ | A | -1' | 28-0 | W | 28 | **W** | **+26'** |
| 1992 | 12 | SUN | PHI | NYG | A | -3' | 47-34 | W | 13 | **W** | **+9'** |
| 1993 | 14 | SUN | OAK | BUF | A | +6' | 25-24 | W | 1 | **W** | **+7'** |
| 1993 | 16 | SUN | SF | DET | A | -9' | 55-17 | W | 38 | **W** | **+28'** |
| 1995 | 8 | SUN | SF | STL | A | -3' | 44-10 | W | 34 | **W** | **+30'** |
| 1995 | 16 | SAT | GB | NO | A | -5' | 34-23 | W | 11 | **W** | **+5'** |
| 1996 | 5 | SUN | GB | SEA | A | -10 | 31-10 | W | 21 | **W** | **+11** |
| 1998 | 6 | SUN | SF | NO | A | -10 | 31-0 | W | 31 | **W** | **+21** |
| 1998 | 12 | SUN | NYJ | TEN | A | +1 | 24-3 | W | 21 | **W** | **+22** |
| 2000 | 9 | SUN | STL | SF | A | -7 | 34-24 | W | 10 | **W** | **+3** |
| 2000 | 10 | SUN | DEN | NYJ | A | +3 | 30-23 | W | 7 | **W** | **+10** |
| 2000 | 17 | SAT | JAC | NYG | A | +4 | 25-28 | L | -3 | **W** | **+1** |
| 2001 | 4 | SUN | BAL | DEN | A | +4' | 20-13 | W | 7 | **W** | **+11'** |
| 2006 | 8 | SUN | JAC | PHI | A | +7' | 13-6 | W | 7 | **W** | **+14'** |
| *2007* | *3* | *SUN* | *CIN* | *SEA* | *A* | *+3'* | *21-24* | *L* | *-3* | ***W*** | ***+0'*** |
| —— | — | —— | —— | —— | — | —— | —— | — | —— | — | —— |
| —— | — | —— | —— | —— | — | —— | —— | — | —— | — | —— |
| —— | — | —— | —— | —— | — | —— | —— | — | —— | — | —— |

# NFL POWER SYSTEM #12

Road favorites are the focus of *Section 12* of the **PRO INFO SPORTS 2008 NFL POWER SYSTEM e-CYCLOPEDIA.** This featured situation has been going strong since 1984, as qualifying teams have failed to beat the spread in 20 games.

Teams finding themselves as a road favorite after pulling off an upset win on the road as a big underdog have failed miserably against opponents not on a long losing streak.

Play **AGAINST** a road favorite/pick 'em off a SU win as a road underdog of more than 5 points in its last game vs. an opponent *not* off 5 SU losses in its last 5 games.

SU: 16-4 (8.1)     **ATS: 19-0-1 (11.0)**

| YEAR | WK | DAY | TEAM | OPP | ST | LINE | SCORE | SU | MRG | ATS | MRG |
|------|----|-----|------|-----|----|------|-------|----|----|-----|-----|
| 1984 | 8 | SUN | NYG | PHI | A | -1 | 10-24 | L | -14 | **L** | **-15** |
| 1984 | 8 | SUN | PIT | IND | A | -5 | 16-17 | L | -1 | **L** | **-6** |
| 1984 | 11 | SUN | NYG | TB | A | -3 | 17-20 | L | -3 | **L** | **-6** |
| 1985 | 16 | SUN | GB | TB | A | -3 | 20-17 | W | 3 | **P** | **0** |
| 1986 | 4 | SUN | ATL | TB | A | -7 | 23-20 | W | 3 | **L** | **-4** |
| 1986 | 10 | SUN | STL | NO | A | -3 | 0-6 | L | -6 | **L** | **-9** |
| 1987 | 6 | SUN | NE | IND | A | -6' | 16-30 | L | -14 | **L** | **-7'** |
| 1987 | 10 | SUN | IND | NE | A | 0 | 0-24 | L | -24 | **L** | **-24** |
| 1990 | 5 | SUN | TB | DAL | A | -2' | 10-14 | L | -4 | **L** | **-6'** |
| 1990 | 11 | SUN | GB | ARZ | A | -5 | 24-21 | W | 3 | **L** | **-2** |
| 1991 | 8 | SUN | ATL | ARZ | A | -2' | 10-16 | L | -6 | **L** | **-8'** |
| 1991 | 17 | SUN | NE | CIN | A | -2 | 7-29 | L | -22 | **L** | **-24** |
| 1993 | 12 | SUN | MIN | TB | A | -7' | 10-23 | L | -13 | **L** | **-20'** |
| 1993 | 16 | SUN | STL | CIN | A | -2 | 3-15 | L | -12 | **L** | **-14** |
| 1997 | 15 | THU | TEN | CIN | A | -2' | 14-41 | L | -27 | **L** | **-29'** |
| 1998 | 10 | SUN | OAK | BAL | A | -1' | 10-13 | L | -3 | **L** | **-4'** |
| 1998 | 15 | SUN | NE | STL | A | -7 | 18-32 | L | -14 | **L** | **-21** |
| 2001 | 13 | SUN | TB | CIN | A | -6 | 16-13 | W | 3 | **L** | **-3** |
| 2004 | 6 | SUN | KC | JAC | A | -2 | 16-22 | L | -6 | **L** | **-8** |
| 2005 | 17 | SUN | BUF | NYJ | A | -1' | 26-30 | L | -4 | **L** | **-5'** |

# NFL POWER SYSTEM #13

We turn our attention to road favorites in *Section 13* of the **PRO INFO SPORTS NFL POWER SYSTEM e-CYCLOPEDIA**. The featured scenario below has cashed in every qualifying game since 1992, beating the spread by more than a dozen ppg on average.

After a pitiful home game with at least a half-dozen turnovers, big road underdogs have continued their poor play under the circumstances described.

Play **ON** a road underdog of 8 points or less/pick 'em off a SU win scoring less than 10 points in its last game vs. an opponent *not* off a non-division home favorite SU loss in its last game.

SU: 13-3 (7.2)     **ATS: 15-0-1 (12.2)**

| YEAR | WK | DAY | TEAM | OPP | ST | LINE | SCORE | SU | MRG | ATS | MRG |
|------|----|----|------|-----|----|------|-------|----|----|-----|-----|
| 1992 | 15 | SUN | IND | NYJ | A | +5 | 10-6 | W | 4 | **W** | **+9** |
| 1993 | 6 | SUN | CHI | PHI | A | +7 | 17-6 | W | 11 | **W** | **+18** |
| 1993 | 10 | SUN | IND | WAS | A | +7 | 24-30 | L | -6 | **W** | **+1** |
| 1993 | 16 | SUN | NE | BAL | A | +6 | 20-17 | W | 3 | **W** | **+9** |
| 1997 | 7 | SUN | CAR | SD | A | 0 | 26-7 | W | 19 | **W** | **+19** |
| 2000 | 2 | SUN | CLE | IND | A | +6' | 38-31 | W | 7 | **W** | **+13'** |
| 2000 | 4 | SUN | GB | ARZ | A | +1' | 29-3 | W | 26 | **W** | **+27'** |
| 2000 | 10 | SUN | PIT | TEN | A | +7' | 7-9 | L | -2 | **W** | **+5'** |
| 2003 | 9 | MON | NE | DEN | A | +2' | 30-26 | W | 4 | **W** | **+6'** |
| 2004 | 3 | SUN | JAC | TEN | A | +6 | 15-12 | W | 3 | **W** | **+9** |
| 2004 | 4 | SUN | ATL | CAR | A | +3' | 27-10 | W | 17 | **W** | **+20'** |
| 2005 | 2 | MON | WAS | DAL | A | +6 | 14-13 | W | 1 | **W** | **+7** |
| 2006 | 3 | SUN | JAC | IND | A | +7 | 14-21 | L | -7 | **P** | **0** |
| 2006 | 3 | SUN | DEN | NE | A | +6' | 17-7 | W | 10 | **W** | **+16'** |
| 2006 | 10 | SUN | SF | DET | A | +6 | 19-13 | W | 6 | **W** | **+12** |
| 2006 | 17 | SUN | GB | CHI | A | +3 | 26-7 | W | 19 | **W** | **+22** |
| —— | — | —— | ———— | ——— | — | ——— | ———— | — | —— | — | —— |
| —— | — | —— | ———— | ——— | — | ——— | ———— | — | —— | — | —— |
| —— | — | —— | ———— | ——— | — | ——— | ———— | — | —— | — | —— |

# NFL POWER SYSTEM #14

Sunday Night Football has increased in prominence and popularity in the NFL, where it is now more of a "big" game than Monday Night Football. *Section 14* of the **PRO INFO SPORTS 2008 NFL POWER SYSTEM e-CYCLOPEDIA** examines various situations in which the league has been perfect in either covering or failing to cover the spread before, during, and after Sunday Night Football games.

Sunday Night teams off a game that followed a bye week have been very flat at home as a favorite or small underdog.

Play **AGAINST** a Sunday Night home team (*not* an underdog of 7+ points) with a TOTAL of 39+ points off a game last week and a BYE before that.

SU: 9-7 (3.5)        **ATS: 15-0-1 (8.5)**

| YEAR | WK | DAY | TEAM | OPP | ST | LINE | SCORE | SU | MRG | ATS | MRG |
|------|----|-----|------|-----|----|------|-------|----|----|-----|-----|
| 1991 | 9  | SNF | NYG  | WAS | H  | +3   | 13-17 | L  | -4  | L   | -1  |
| 1993 | 5  | SNF | BUF  | NYG | H  | -5   | 17-14 | W  | 3   | L   | -2  |
| 1994 | 6  | SNF | PHI  | WAS | H  | -13  | 21-17 | W  | 4   | L   | -9  |
| 1994 | 13 | SNF | IND  | NE  | H  | 0    | 10-12 | L  | -2  | L   | -2  |
| 1995 | 6  | SNF | NE   | DEN | H  | -4   | 3-37  | L  | -34 | L   | -38 |
| 1995 | 10 | SNF | SD   | MIA | H  | -1'  | 14-24 | L  | -10 | L   | -11'|
| 1996 | 4  | SNF | ATL  | PHI | H  | -2'  | 18-33 | L  | -15 | L   | -17'|
| 1996 | 6  | SNF | CIN  | TEN | H  | 0    | 27-30 | L  | -3  | L   | -3  |
| 1996 | 7  | SNF | IND  | BAL | H  | -8   | 26-21 | W  | 5   | L   | -3  |
| 1997 | 10 | SNF | GB   | DET | H  | -10  | 20-10 | W  | 10  | P   | 0   |
| 1998 | 9  | SNF | SEA  | OAK | H  | -7   | 18-31 | L  | -13 | L   | -20 |
| 1999 | 5  | SNF | GB   | TB  | H  | -5   | 26-23 | W  | 3   | L   | -2  |
| 2001 | 6  | SNF | IND  | OAK | H  | -3'  | 18-23 | L  | -5  | L   | -8' |
| 2003 | 6  | SNF | SEA  | SF  | H  | -3'  | 20-19 | W  | 1   | L   | -2' |
| 2004 | 12 | SNF | DEN  | OAK | H  | -11  | 24-25 | L  | -1  | L   | -12 |
| 2005 | 8  | SNF | NE   | BUF | H  | -9   | 21-16 | W  | 5   | L   | -4  |
| ____ | _  | ____ | ____ | ____ | _ | ____ | ____ | _ | ___ | _ | ___ |
| ____ | _  | ____ | ____ | ____ | _ | ____ | ____ | _ | ___ | _ | ___ |
| ____ | _  | ____ | ____ | ____ | _ | ____ | ____ | _ | ___ | _ | ___ |

# NFL POWER SYSTEM #15

We have so many systems revolving around Monday Night Football that we devote an entire chapter *(Section 15)* of the **PRO INFO SPORTS 2008 NFL e-CYCLOPEDIA** just to how teams perform *before* and *after* such an appearance. This featured **POWER SYSTEM** reveals with 2 more wins last season, how strongly teams have done after playing on Monday under certain conditions.

Following a strong showing as a Monday road favorite, teams have returned home and taken care of business against non-division opponents.

Play **ON** a non-division home team with a TOTAL of 36-48 points or less off a Monday road favorite SU win in its last game vs. an opponent *not* a home favorite in its last 2 games.

SU: 13-0 (19.7)        **ATS: 13-0 (11.2)**

| YEAR | WK | DAY | TEAM | OPP | ST | LINE | SCORE | SU | MRG | ATS | MRG |
|------|----|-----|------|-----|----|------|-------|----|----|-----|-----|
| 1989 | 15 | SUN | SF | BUF | H | -5 | 21-10 | W | 11 | **W** | **+6** |
| 1990 | 2 | SUN | SF | WAS | H | -4' | 26-13 | W | 13 | **W** | **+8'** |
| 1990 | 15 | SUN | OAK | CIN | H | -7 | 24-7 | W | 17 | **W** | **+10** |
| 1992 | 3 | SUN | MIA | STL | H | -8' | 26-10 | W | 16 | **W** | **+7'** |
| 1992 | 12 | SUN | BUF | ATL | H | -14 | 41-14 | W | 27 | **W** | **+13** |
| 1992 | 17 | SUN | DAL | CHI | H | -11' | 27-14 | W | 13 | **W** | **+1'** |
| 1999 | 4 | SUN | SF | TEN | H | -1 | 24-22 | W | 2 | **W** | **+1** |
| 2003 | 5 | SUN | GB | SEA | H | -1' | 35-13 | W | 22 | **W** | **+20'** |
| 2003 | 8 | SUN | KC | BUF | H | -6 | 38-5 | W | 33 | **W** | **+27** |
| 2003 | 17 | SUN | GB | DEN | H | -7 | 31-3 | W | 28 | **W** | **+21** |
| 2004 | 12 | SUN | NE | BAL | H | -7 | 24-3 | W | 21 | **W** | **+14** |
| 2006 | 8 | SUN | CHI | SF | H | -16' | 41-10 | W | 31 | **W** | **+14'** |
| *2007* | *5* | *SUN* | *NE* | *CLE* | *H* | *-16'* | *34-17* | *W* | *17* | *W* | *+0'* |
| *2007* | *7* | *SUN* | *NYG* | *SF* | *H* | *-9'* | *33-15* | *W* | *18* | *W* | *+8'* |
| —— | — | —— | ———— | ———— | — | —— | ———— | — | —— | — | —— |
| —— | — | —— | ———— | ———— | — | —— | ———— | — | —— | — | —— |
| —— | — | —— | ———— | ———— | — | —— | ———— | — | —— | — | —— |

# NFL POWER SYSTEM #16

Due to changes in the NFL, some older Monday Night Football situations are no longer valid, while others have developed recently. Our featured Monday Night Football scenario from *Section 16* of the **PRO INFO SPORTS 2008 NFL POWER SYSTEM e-CYCLOPEDIA** is perfect since 1998, crushing the spread by 2 TDs per game on average.

After tossing 3 or more interceptions, teams have struggled on Monday Night Football.

Play **AGAINST** a Monday underdog off a SU loss with 3+ interceptions thrown vs. an opponent *not* off a favorite ATS loss in its last game.

SU: 13-0 (20.8)     **ATS: 13-0 (13.7)**

| YEAR | WK | DAY | TEAM | OPP | ST | LINE | SCORE | SU | MRG | ATS | MRG |
|------|-----|------|------|------|-----|------|-------|-----|------|------|------|
| 1998 | 11 | MON | KC | DEN | H | +4 | 7-30 | L | -23 | L | -19 |
| 1999 | 3 | MON | ARZ | *SF* | H | +2 | 10-24 | L | -14 | L | -12 |
| 1999 | 12 | MON | *SF* | GB | H | +6 | 3-20 | L | -17 | L | -11 |
| 2000 | 7 | MON | JAC | TEN | A | +6' | 13-27 | L | -14 | L | -7' |
| 2000 | 15 | MON | BUF | IND | A | +6 | 20-44 | L | -24 | L | -18 |
| 2001 | 5 | MON | DET | STL | H | +12 | 0-35 | L | -35 | L | -23 |
| 2001 | 18 | MON | MIN | BAL | A | +11' | 3-19 | L | -16 | L | -4' |
| 2002 | 9 | MON | MIA | GB | A | +4' | 10-24 | L | -14 | L | -9' |
| 2004 | 10 | MON | DAL | PHI | H | +6' | 21-49 | L | -28 | L | -21' |
| 2004 | 12 | MON | STL | GB | A | +6' | 17-45 | L | -28 | L | -21' |
| 2005 | 14 | MON | NO | ATL | A | +10' | 17-36 | L | -19 | L | -8' |
| 2006 | 14 | MON | ARZ | CHI | H | +6' | 27-42 | L | -15 | L | -8' |
| *2007* | *10* | *MON* | *SF* | *SEA* | *A* | *+10* | *0-24* | *L* | *-24* | *L* | *-14* |
| —— | – | —— | —— | —— | – | —— | —— | – | —— | – | —— |
| —— | – | —— | —— | —— | – | —— | —— | – | —— | – | —— |
| —— | – | —— | —— | —— | – | —— | —— | – | —— | – | —— |

# NFL POWER SYSTEM #17

Besides Sunday, Sunday Night Football, and Monday Night Football, there are occasional games on other days of the week in the NFL. *Section 17* of the **PRO INFO SPORTS POWER SYSTEM e-CYCLOPEDIA** examines how teams do in various non-Sunday situations. The scenario we reveal here has been perfect SU & ATS since the early 1990s and enjoyed an easy 16-point spread win last year.

Despite covering the spread in an earlier defeat, non-Sunday teams playing with revenge have been perfectly dreadful.

Play **AGAINST** a non-Sunday/non-Thursday team seeking revenge for a SU loss and ATS win, allowing less than 37 points in the first matchup.

SU: 16-0 (16.6)      **ATS: 16-0 (12.0)**

| YEAR | WK | DAY | TEAM | OPP | ST | LINE | SCORE | SU | MRG | ATS | MRG |
|------|----|----|------|-----|----|------|-------|----|-----|-----|-----|
| 1991 | 12 | MON | MIA | BUF | H | +4 | 27-41 | L | -14 | L | -10 |
| 1991 | 16 | SAT | TB | CHI | A | +13' | 0-27 | L | -27 | L | -13' |
| 1992 | 9 | MON | CHI | MIN | H | -3' | 10-38 | L | -28 | L | -31' |
| 1993 | 8 | MON | CHI | MIN | H | -3 | 12-19 | L | -7 | L | -10 |
| 1994 | 13 | MON | NO | SF | H | +9' | 14-35 | L | -21 | L | -11' |
| 1995 | 17 | MON | ARZ | DAL | H | +9 | 13-37 | L | -24 | L | -15 |
| 1995 | 17 | SAT | TB | DET | H | +7' | 10-37 | L | -27 | L | -19' |
| 1997 | 17 | MON | MIA | NE | H | -3 | 12-14 | L | -2 | L | -5 |
| 2003 | 17 | SAT | SF | SEA | H | -2 | 17-24 | L | -7 | L | -9 |
| 2003 | 17 | SAT | WAS | PHI | H | +7' | 7-31 | L | -24 | L | -16' |
| 2004 | 16 | FRI | MIN | GB | H | -3 | 31-34 | L | -3 | L | -6 |
| 2005 | 14 | MON | NO | ATL | A | +10' | 17-36 | L | -19 | L | -8' |
| 2005 | 16 | SAT | HOU | JAC | H | +6' | 20-38 | L | -18 | L | -11' |
| 2006 | 10 | MON | TB | CAR | A | +10 | 10-24 | L | -14 | L | -4 |
| 2006 | 16 | SAT | OAK | KC | H | +7 | 9-20 | L | -11 | L | -4 |
| *2007* | *14* | *MON* | *ATL* | *NO* | *H* | *+4* | *14-34* | *L* | *-20* | *L* | *-16* |

# NFL POWER SYSTEM #18

In *Section 18* of the **2008 NFL POWER SYSTEM e-CYCLOPEDIA, PRO INFO SPORTS** investigates many *Revenge* scenarios. In this featured situation, small home dogs have not only covered the spread under the conditions described, but have won every game outright by double digits on average since the late 1980s.

From the 6th game of the season on, small home underdogs have been strong when looking to avenge a loss of 6+ points and turning the ball over numerous times.

From **Game 6 on,** play **ON** a home underdog of less than 3 points/pick 'em seeking revenge for a SU loss of 6+ points with 3+ turnovers in the first matchup 5+ games ago.

SU: 13-0 (11.5)      **ATS: 13-0 (13.1)**

| YEAR | WK | DAY | TEAM | OPP | ST | LINE | SCORE | SU | MRG | ATS | MRG |
|------|----|-----|------|-----|----|------|-------|----|----|-----|-----|
| 1989 | 15 | SUN | IND | MIA | H | 0 | 42-13 | W | 29 | W | +29 |
| 1990 | 16 | SUN | CIN | TEN | H | +2' | 40-20 | W | 20 | W | +22' |
| 1990 | 17 | SUN | TEN | PIT | H | +2 | 34-14 | W | 20 | W | +22 |
| 1994 | 17 | SAT | NYG | DAL | H | +2 | 15-10 | W | 5 | W | +7 |
| 1995 | 13 | MON | SD | OAK | H | +1 | 12-6 | W | 6 | W | +7 |
| 1998 | 9 | SUN | WAS | NYG | H | +2' | 21-14 | W | 7 | W | +9' |
| 1999 | 10 | SUN | NO | SF | H | +1 | 24-6 | W | 18 | W | +19 |
| 1999 | 11 | SUN | ARZ | DAL | H | +2 | 13-9 | W | 4 | W | +6 |
| 1999 | 17 | SUN | BUF | IND | H | +2 | 31-6 | W | 25 | W | +27 |
| 2001 | 15 | SUN | KC | DEN | H | +1 | 26-23 | W | 3 | W | +4 |
| 2002 | 17 | SUN | NE | MIA | H | +1 | 27-24 | W | 3 | W | +4 |
| 2005 | 17 | SUN | NYJ | BUF | H | +1' | 30-26 | W | 4 | W | +5' |
| *2007* | *16* | *SUN* | *CIN* | *CLE* | *H* | *+2'* | *19-14* | *W* | *5* | *W* | *+7'* |
| ____ | _ | ___ | ____ | ____ | _ | ____ | _____ | _ | ___ | _ | ___ |
| ____ | _ | ___ | ____ | ____ | _ | ____ | _____ | _ | ___ | _ | ___ |
| ____ | _ | ___ | ____ | ____ | _ | ____ | _____ | _ | ___ | _ | ___ |

# NFL POWER SYSTEM #19

Shutouts are a relatively rare occurrence in the NFL. **PRO INFO SPORTS** research reveals that teams coming off a shutout game, regardless of which end they were on, have reacted strongly the next time out. These situations are detailed in *Section 19* of the **2008 NFL POWER SYSTEM e-CYCLOPEDIA,** including the following featured scenario that has been perfect SU & ATS for well over 20 seasons.

After blanking a conference opponent at home and scoring at least 4 TDs worth of points, favorites have been rock solid for 20+ seasons.

Play **ON** a non-Monday favorite/pick 'em off a conference home shutout SU win, scoring 28+ points last week.

SU: 15-0 (17.9)      **ATS: 15-0 (10.5)**

| YEAR | WK | DAY | TEAM | OPP | ST | LINE | SCORE | SU | MRG | ATS | MRG |
|------|----|-----|------|-----|----|----|-------|----|-----|-----|-----|
| 1985 | 4  | SUN | MIA | DEN | A | -1 | 30-26 | W | 4 | **W** | **+3** |
| 1987 | 15 | SUN | SF | ATL | H | -16 | 35-7 | W | 28 | **W** | **+12** |
| 1991 | 4  | SUN | WAS | CIN | A | -4 | 34-27 | W | 7 | **W** | **+3** |
| 1992 | 4  | SUN | BUF | NE | A | -16 | 41-7 | W | 34 | **W** | **+18** |
| 1993 | 18 | SUN | NE | MIA | H | 0 | 33-27 | W | 6 | **W** | **+6** |
| 1997 | 12 | SUN | PIT | CIN | H | -8' | 20-3 | W | 17 | **W** | **+8'** |
| 1997 | 16 | SUN | KC | SD | A | -9' | 29-7 | W | 22 | **W** | **+12'** |
| 2000 | 3  | SUN | TB | DET | A | -3 | 31-10 | W | 21 | **W** | **+18** |
| 2000 | 5  | SUN | BAL | CLE | A | -8' | 12-0 | W | 12 | **W** | **+3'** |
| 2000 | 15 | SUN | JAC | ARZ | H | -16 | 44-10 | W | 34 | **W** | **+18** |
| 2001 | 4  | SUN | GB | CAR | A | -4 | 28-7 | W | 21 | **W** | **+17** |
| 2003 | 2  | SUN | BUF | JAC | A | -3 | 38-17 | W | 21 | **W** | **+18** |
| 2003 | 7  | SUN | STL | GB | H | -4 | 34-24 | W | 10 | **W** | **+6** |
| 2005 | 9  | SUN | NYG | SF | A | -10' | 24-6 | W | 18 | **W** | **+7'** |
| *2007* | *11* | *SUN* | *GB* | *CAR* | *H* | *-10* | *31-17* | *W* | *14* | ***W*** | ***+7*** |

# NFL POWER SYSTEM #20

Overtime games are another somewhat rare event in the NFL. Regardless of which end they were on after going into a 5th quarter, our research shows that such teams have reacted consistently the next time out under certain conditions. These situations are detailed in *Section 20* of the **PRO INFO SPORTS 2008 NFL POWER SYSTEM e-CYCLOPEDIA,** including the following featured scenario that has been perfect since at least 1980, beating the spread 19 straight times.

After a tough, defensive brawl in which they scored less than 20 points in OT, home underdogs of less than a TD have been very strong for 25+ seasons.

From **Game 4 on,** play **ON** a home underdog of less than 7 points with a TOTAL of 34½-43 points off an OT contest scoring less than 20 points in its last game.

SU: 15-4 (9.7)          **ATS: 19-0 (12.3)**

| YEAR | WK | DAY | TEAM | OPP | ST | LINE | SCORE | SU | MRG | ATS | MRG |
|------|----|-----|------|-----|-----|------|-------|-----|-----|-----|------|
| 1980 | 16 | SUN | CIN | BAL | H | +3' | 24-27 | L | -3 | **W** | **+0'** |
| 1985 | 11 | SUN | ATL | STL | H | +6' | 30-14 | W | 16 | **W** | **+22'** |
| 1985 | 13 | THU | DET | NYJ | H | +3 | 31-20 | W | 11 | **W** | **+14** |
| 1987 | 11 | SUN | NE | IND | H | 0 | 24-0 | W | 24 | **W** | **+24** |
| 1989 | 12 | SUN | KC | TEN | H | +1 | 34-0 | W | 34 | **W** | **+35** |
| 1990 | 13 | SUN | SEA | TEN | H | +2 | 13-10 | W | 3 | **W** | **+5** |
| 1991 | 5 | SUN | NYJ | MIA | H | +1' | 41-23 | W | 18 | **W** | **+19'** |
| 1991 | 16 | SUN | SD | MIA | H | +1 | 38-30 | W | 8 | **W** | **+9** |
| 1995 | 10 | SUN | SEA | NYG | H | 0 | 30-28 | W | 2 | **W** | **+2** |
| 1996 | 13 | SUN | MIN | DEN | H | +5 | 17-21 | L | -4 | **W** | **+1** |
| 1996 | 15 | THU | IND | PHI | H | +4' | 37-10 | W | 27 | **W** | **+31'** |
| 1997 | 13 | SUN | PHI | PIT | H | +3 | 23-20 | W | 3 | **W** | **+6** |
| 1999 | 17 | SUN | BUF | IND | H | +2 | 31-6 | W | 25 | **W** | **+27** |
| 1999 | 17 | SUN | NE | BAL | H | +2 | 20-3 | W | 17 | **W** | **+19** |
| 2000 | 17 | SUN | NE | MIA | H | +4' | 24-27 | L | -3 | **W** | **+1'** |
| 2001 | 8 | SUN | CAR | NYJ | H | +2' | 12-13 | L | -1 | **W** | **+1'** |
| 2003 | 7 | SUN | CIN | BAL | H | +1 | 34-26 | W | 8 | **W** | **+9** |
| 2003 | 9 | SUN | ARZ | CIN | H | +2' | 17-14 | W | 3 | **W** | **+5'** |
| *2006* | *3* | *SUN* | *MIN* | *CHI* | *H* | *+3'* | *16-19* | *L* | *-3* | ***W*** | ***+0'*** |
| —— | — | —— | —— | —— | — | —— | —— | — | — | — | —— |
| —— | — | —— | —— | —— | — | —— | —— | — | — | — | —— |
| —— | — | —— | —— | —— | — | —— | —— | — | — | — | —— |

# NFL POWER SYSTEM #21

Ever since the NFL added *byes* to the schedule, **PRO INFO SPORTS** has followed how teams have done both *before* and *after* a week of rest. Our research is revealed in *Section 21* of the **2008 NFL POWER SYSTEM e-CYCLOPEDIA,** and we feature one of those very strong situations below that has produced 18 straight winners.

Play **AGAINST** a division favorite of more than 1 point with a TOTAL under 46 points off a BYE and a road SU loss of 4+ points in its last game.

SU: 11-7 (3.6)          **ATS: 18-0 (9.7)**

| YEAR | WK | DAY | TEAM | OPP | ST | LINE | SCORE | SU | MRG | ATS | MRG |
|------|----|-----|------|-----|----|------|-------|----|-----|-----|-----|
| 1990 | 15 | SUN | NYJ | IND | H | -3' | 21-29 | L | -8 | **L** | **-11'** |
| 1991 | 7 | SUN | SF | ATL | H | -10 | 34-39 | L | -5 | **L** | **-15** |
| 1992 | 6 | SUN | PIT | CLE | A | -3 | 9-17 | L | -8 | **L** | **-11** |
| 1992 | 8 | MON | BUF | NYJ | A | -9' | 24-20 | W | 4 | **L** | **-5'** |
| 1992 | 9 | SUN | ATL | STL | H | -3' | 30-28 | W | 2 | **L** | **-1'** |
| 1993 | 10 | SUN | PIT | CIN | A | -10' | 24-16 | W | 8 | **L** | **-2'** |
| 1993 | 11 | SUN | STL | ATL | H | -4 | 0-13 | L | -13 | **L** | **-17** |
| 1995 | 8 | SUN | CLE | JAC | H | -13' | 15-23 | L | -8 | **L** | **-21'** |
| 1995 | 8 | THU | PIT | CIN | H | -8' | 9-27 | L | -18 | **L** | **-26'** |
| 1996 | 8 | MON | SD | OAK | H | -3' | 14-23 | L | -9 | **L** | **-12'** |
| 1996 | 9 | MON | MIN | CHI | H | -6' | 13-15 | L | -2 | **L** | **-8'** |
| 1996 | 11 | SUN | JAC | BAL | H | -4 | 30-27 | W | 3 | **L** | **-1** |
| 2000 | 5 | SUN | BUF | IND | H | -2 | 16-18 | L | -2 | **L** | **-4** |
| 2000 | 8 | THU | TB | DET | H | -8 | 14-28 | L | -14 | **L** | **-22** |
| 2000 | 10 | SUN | NE | BUF | H | -2 | 13-16 | L | -3 | **L** | **-5** |
| 2001 | 9 | SUN | GB | TB | H | -5' | 21-20 | W | 1 | **L** | **-4'** |
| 2005 | 8 | SUN | NE | BUF | H | -9 | 21-16 | W | 5 | **L** | **-4** |
| 2006 | 6 | SUN | SEA | STL | A | -3 | 30-28 | W | 2 | **L** | **-1** |
| ___ | _ | ___ | ___ | ___ | _ | ___ | ___ | _ | ___ | _ | ___ |
| ___ | _ | ___ | ___ | ___ | _ | ___ | ___ | _ | ___ | _ | ___ |
| ___ | _ | ___ | ___ | ___ | _ | ___ | ___ | _ | ___ | _ | ___ |

# NFL POWER SYSTEM #22

In *Section 22* of the **2008 NFL POWER SYSTEM e-CYCLOPEDIA, PRO INFO SPORTS** examines how the rest of the league does *before* playing certain teams. In some of these situations, *where* the game is being played is part of the equation as well. Such is the case with the following featured system.

*Before* going to Jacksonville, teams at the right price have been very focused in recent seasons.

Play **ON** a non-Saturday team (*not* a favorite of more than 5 points *or* underdog of more than 15 points) before a non-Monday game at **Jacksonville**.

SU: 13-4 (8.0)          **ATS: 17-0 (10.6)**

| YEAR | WK | DAY | TEAM | OPP | ST | LINE | SCORE | SU | MRG | ATS | MRG |
|------|----|-----|------|-----|----|----|-------|----|----|-----|-----|
| 2002 | 9  | SUN | WAS  | SEA | A  | +2' | 14-3  | W  | 11 | W   | +13' |
| 2002 | 15 | MON | TEN  | NE  | H  | -2' | 24-7  | W  | 17 | W   | +14' |
| 2003 | 1  | SUN | BUF  | NE  | H  | -1  | 31-0  | W  | 31 | W   | +30 |
| 2003 | 4  | SUN | SD   | OAK | A  | +7  | 31-34 | L  | -3 | W   | +4  |
| 2003 | 5  | SUN | MIA  | NYG | A  | +1  | 23-10 | W  | 13 | W   | +14 |
| 2003 | 7  | SUN | TEN  | CAR | A  | +1  | 37-17 | W  | 20 | W   | +21 |
| 2003 | 9  | SUN | IND  | MIA | A  | +3  | 23-17 | W  | 6  | W   | +9  |
| 2003 | 13 | SUN | HOU  | ATL | H  | -3  | 17-13 | W  | 4  | W   | +1  |
| 2004 | 1  | SUN | DEN  | KC  | H  | -3  | 34-24 | W  | 10 | W   | +7  |
| 2004 | 3  | SUN | IND  | GB  | H  | -6' | 45-31 | W  | 14 | W   | +7' |
| 2004 | 4  | MON | KC   | BAL | A  | +5' | 27-24 | W  | 3  | W   | +8' |
| 2004 | 13 | SUN | CHI  | MIN | A  | +7  | 24-24 | W  | 10 | W   | +17 |
| 2005 | 3  | MON | HOU  | KC  | H  | -3  | 30-10 | W  | 20 | W   | +17 |
| 2006 | 4  | SUN | NYJ  | IND | H  | +8  | 28-31 | L  | -3 | W   | +5  |
| 2006 | 8  | SUN | TEN  | HOU | H  | -3  | 28-22 | W  | 6  | W   | +3  |
| 2006 | 9  | SUN | HOU  | NYG | A  | +12' | 10-14 | L | -4 | W   | +8' |
| 2007 | 10 | SUN | SD   | IND | H  | +3' | 23-21 | W  | 2  | W   | +5' |
| 2007 | 15 | SUN | OAK  | IND | H  | +9' | 14-21 | L  | -7 | W   | +2' |
| —— | — | —— | —— | —— | — | —— | —— | — | — | — | —— |
| —— | — | —— | —— | —— | — | —— | —— | — | — | — | —— |
| —— | — | —— | —— | —— | — | —— | —— | — | — | — | —— |

# NFL POWER SYSTEM #23

*Section 23* of **PRO INFO SPORTS 2008 NFL POWER SYSTEM e-CYCLOPEDIA** continues our examination of how the league reacts to games against specific opponents. The featured situation below involving how teams do after a road game against the Cowboys has been very strong in recent seasons, including last year's spread win of 24+ points.

In a very simple situation following a game at Dallas, home favorites have been big disappointments for their backers in recent years.

Play **AGAINST** a conference home favorite off a non-Monday contest at **Dallas** in its last game.

SU: 13-1 (7.3)　　　**ATS: 14-0 (11.9)**

| YEAR | WK | DAY | TEAM | OPP | ST | LINE | SCORE | SU | MRG | ATS | MRG |
|------|----|-----|------|-----|----|----|-------|----|----|-----|------|
| 2001 | 12 | SUN | PHI | WAS | H | -8' | 3-13 | L | -10 | L | -18' |
| 2001 | 15 | SAT | NYG | ARZ | H | -5 | 17-13 | W | 4 | L | -1 |
| 2002 | 3 | SUN | TEN | CLE | H | -4 | 28-31 | L | -3 | L | -7 |
| 2002 | 6 | SUN | NYG | ATL | H | -5 | 10-17 | L | -7 | L | -12 |
| 2002 | 9 | SUN | SEA | WAS | H | -2' | 3-14 | L | -11 | L | -13' |
| 2002 | 14 | SUN | WAS | NYG | H | -2' | 21-27 | L | -6 | L | -8' |
| 2002 | 15 | SUN | SF | GB | H | -3 | 14-20 | L | -6 | L | -9 |
| 2003 | 2 | SUN | ATL | WAS | H | -3 | 31-33 | L | -2 | L | -5 |
| 2003 | 11 | SUN | BUF | HOU | H | -7 | 10-12 | L | -2 | L | -9 |
| 2003 | 13 | SUN | CAR | PHI | H | -1 | 16-25 | L | -9 | L | -10 |
| 2004 | 7 | SUN | NYG | DET | H | -7 | 13-28 | L | -15 | L | -22 |
| 2004 | 9 | SUN | DET | WAS | H | -3' | 10-17 | L | -7 | L | -10' |
| 2006 | 15 | SUN | NO | WAS | H | -9' | 10-16 | L | -6 | L | -15' |
| *2007* | *2* | *SUN* | *NYG* | *GB* | *H* | *-2'* | *13-35* | *L* | *-22* | *L* | *-24'* |
| ___ | _ | ___ | ___ | ___ | _ | ___ | ___ | _ | ___ | _ | ___ |
| ___ | _ | ___ | ___ | ___ | _ | ___ | ___ | _ | ___ | _ | ___ |
| ___ | _ | ___ | ___ | ___ | _ | ___ | ___ | _ | ___ | _ | ___ |

# NFL POWER SYSTEM #24

*Section 24* of **PRO INFO SPORTS 2008 NFL e-CYCLOPEDIA** is our collection of all other miscellaneous regular season **POWER SYSTEMS** that don't fit into any of the previous sections. The following featured situation applies to all teams, home or away, favorite or underdog, and has been perfect since at least 1985.

Teams off 2 dominant wins scoring at least 30 points and allowing less than 2 TDs have flopped against non-division opponents.

From **Game 4 on,** play **AGAINST** a non-division team with a TOTAL under 47 points off scoring 30+ points and allowing less than 14 points in its last 2 games.

SU: 11-8 (1.7)          **ATS: 19-0 (9.4)**

| YEAR | WK | DAY | TEAM | OPP | ST | LINE | SCORE | SU | MRG | ATS | MRG |
|------|----|-----|------|-----|----|----|----|----|----|----|----|
| 1985 | 13 | MON | CHI | MIA | A | -3' | 24-38 | L | -14 | L | -17' |
| 1986 | 15 | SUN | MIN | TEN | A | -7' | 10-23 | L | -13 | L | -20' |
| 1989 | 11 | SUN | SF | GB | H | -10' | 17-21 | L | -4 | L | -14' |
| 1992 | 6 | SUN | PHI | KC | A | -2 | 17-24 | L | -7 | L | -9 |
| 1992 | 11 | SUN | MIN | TEN | H | -6' | 13-17 | L | -4 | L | -10' |
| 1993 | 14 | SUN | SF | CIN | H | -23' | 21-8 | W | 13 | L | -10' |
| 1996 | 7 | MON | GB | SF | H | -6 | 23-20 | W | 3 | L | -3 |
| 1996 | 16 | SUN | NE | DAL | A | +5' | 6-12 | L | -6 | L | -0' |
| 1999 | 8 | SUN | STL | TEN | A | -3 | 21-24 | L | -3 | L | -6 |
| 1999 | 9 | SUN | KC | IND | A | +4 | 17-25 | L | -8 | L | -4 |
| 1999 | 17 | SUN | STL | PHI | A | -8 | 31-38 | L | -7 | L | -15 |
| 2000 | 4 | SUN | TB | NYJ | H | -7 | 17-21 | L | -4 | L | -11 |
| 2001 | 6 | SUN | STL | NYG | H | -10' | 15-14 | W | 1 | L | -9' |
| 2002 | 4 | SUN | PHI | HOU | H | -19' | 35-17 | W | 18 | L | -1' |
| 2003 | 4 | SUN | DEN | DET | H | -12 | 20-16 | W | 4 | L | -8 |
| 2003 | 15 | SUN | BAL | OAK | A | -6 | 12-20 | L | -8 | L | -14 |
| 2005 | 15 | SUN | SEA | TEN | A | -7 | 28-24 | W | 4 | L | -3 |
| 2006 | 6 | MON | CHI | ARZ | A | -11' | 24-23 | W | 1 | L | -10' |
| *2007* | *5* | *MON* | *DAL* | *BUF* | *A* | *-10* | *25-24* | *W* | *1* | *L* | *-9* |

# NFL POWER SYSTEM #25

*Section 25* of the **PRO INFO SPORTS 2008 NFL e-CYCLOPEDIA** is exclusive to the playoffs, with situations ranging from WildCard games to the Super Bowl. Of course, the sample of post-season games is much smaller than that of the regular season, but this featured Playoff **POWER SYSTEM** has produced a dozen straight spread wins over the past 25+ seasons.

Playoff road teams well-rested off 2 home wins under the conditions described have been very strong and pulled off many upsets.

Play **ON** a **Playoff** road team off a Playoff home favorite SU win in its last game and a Sunday non-division home favorite SU win before that.

SU: 8-4 (6.3)          **ATS: 12-0 (10.9)**

| SEA | RND | DAY | TEAM | OPP | ST | LINE | SCORE | SU | MRG | ATS | MRG |
|-----|-----|-----|------|-----|-----|------|-------|-----|-----|-----|------|
| 1983 | SF | SAT | SEA | MIA | A | +8 | 27-20 | W | 7 | **W** | **+15** |
| 1992 | CC | SUN | DAL | SF | A | +3' | 34-20 | W | 14 | **W** | **+17'** |
| 1994 | SF | SUN | MIA | SD | A | +2 | 21-22 | L | -1 | **W** | **+1** |
| 1995 | SF | SAT | GB | SF | A | +10 | 27-17 | W | 10 | **W** | **+20** |
| 1997 | CC | SUN | GB | SF | A | -2' | 23-10 | W | 13 | **W** | **+10'** |
| 1998 | CC | SUN | ATL | MIN | A | +10' | 30-27 | W | 3 | **W** | **+13'** |
| 1999 | SF | SAT | WAS | TB | A | +5 | 13-14 | L | -1 | **W** | **+4** |
| 2000 | SF | SUN | BAL | TEN | A | +6 | 24-10 | W | 14 | **W** | **+20** |
| 2003 | SF | SUN | GB | PHI | A | +5' | 17-20 | L | -3 | **W** | **+2'** |
| 2004 | CC | SUN | NE | PIT | A | -3 | 41-27 | W | 14 | **W** | **+11** |
| 2006 | SF | SAT | IND | BAL | A | 4 | 15-6 | W | 9 | **W** | **+13** |
| 2006 | SF | SAT | PHI | NO | A | 5' | 24-27 | L | -3 | **W** | **+2'** |

## UNDERSTANDING & USING NCAA FOOTBALL POWER SYSTEMS

The NCAA Football **POWER SYSTEMS** follow the same basic format as the NFL **POWER SYSTEMS**, with one major exception. Instead of "WK" for "WEEK" number in the charts, "GM" is used for "GAME" number. This is due to college teams not having standardized scheduling.

In the NFL, every team opens the season the same week, plays 16 games, and has one bye during the regular season. Meanwhile, NCAA Football teams don't all begin play the same week, don't all play the same number of games, and some have more than 1 bye while others don't have any; therefore, *game* number is much more useful than *week* number when examining NCAA Football **POWER SYSTEMS**.

The NCAA Football team abbreviations, like the NFL, are common for the most part and should be obvious to college football fans.

Send your **POWER SYSTEM** questions and comments to: **WIN@ProInfoSports.com**.

# NCAA FOOTBALL POWER SYSTEM #1

*Section 1* of the **PRO INFO SPORTS 2008 NCAA FOOTBALL POWER SYSTEM e-CYCLOPEDIA** looks exclusively at season openers. The situation we reveal here has been producing winners for over 20 seasons. While the number of wins is not huge, the average margin is, as teams have obliterated the spread by more than 17 ppg. That's the equivalent of a FG underdog, whipping a favorite by 2 TDs.

After losing a Bowl game in which they were favored by more than a TD, teams have been hungry and determined to start the season off in a big way in front of their home fans.

In **Game 1,** play **ON** a home team (*not* a favorite of 35+ points) off a Bowl Game SU loss as a favorite of more than 7 points last season vs. an opponent at home in its next game.

SU: 11-1 (26.0)     **ATS: 12-0 (17.2)**

| YEAR | GM | DAY | TEAM | OPP | ST | LINE | SCORE | SU | MRG | ATS | MRG |
|------|----|-----|------|-----|----|------|-------|----|----|-----|-----|
| 1984 | 1 | SAT | NEB | WYO | H | -21 | 42-7 | W | 35 | W | +14 |
| 1984 | 1 | SAT | TEX | AUB | H | +2 | 35-27 | W | 8 | W | +10 |
| 1991 | 1 | SAT | OHST | ARZ | H | -8 | 38-14 | W | 24 | W | +16 |
| 1991 | 1 | SAT | ORE | WAST | H | -8 | 40-14 | W | 26 | W | +18 |
| 1992 | 1 | SAT | MIS | AUB | H | +5 | 45-21 | W | 24 | W | +29 |
| 1999 | 1 | SAT | SMIS | TLN | H | -10 | 48-14 | W | 34 | W | +24 |
| 1999 | 1 | SAT | UCLA | BOIS | H | -27 | 38-7 | W | 31 | W | +4 |
| 2003 | 1 | MON | CIN | ECAR | H | -8 | 40-3 | W | 37 | W | +29 |
| 2004 | 1 | SAT | TEX | NTX | H | -26 | 65-0 | W | 65 | W | +39 |
| 2006 | 1 | SAT | AUB | WAST | H | -14' | 40-14 | W | 26 | W | +11' |
| 2006 | 1 | SAT | GTCH | NOTD | H | +7 | 10-14 | L | -4 | W | +3 |
| *2007* | *1* | *MON* | *CLEM* | *FLST* | *H* | *+3* | *24-18* | *W* | *6* | *W* | *+9* |

# NCAA FOOTBALL POWER SYSTEM #2

Continuing with our examination of how college teams do in different parts of the season, *Section 2* of the **PRO INFO SPORTS 2008 NCAA FOOTBALL POWER SYSTEM e-CYCLOPEDIA** examines how teams do in the first half of the season. The featured system below has been very strong over the past 15+ seasons, including crushing the spread by more than 16 ppg on average.

Teams that have recovered from 2 season-opening losses to get back to .500% have been very strong as home/neutral site underdog.

In **Game 5,** play **ON** a .500% home/neutral site underdog/pick 'em off 2 SU wins vs. an opponent *not* a road favorite in its last game.

SU: 10-4 (6.1)          **ATS: 14-0 (16.2)**

| YEAR | GM | DAY | TEAM | OPP | ST | LINE | SCORE | SU | MRG | ATS | MRG |
|------|----|----|------|------|----|------|-------|----|----|-----|-----|
| 1992 | 5 | SAT | TEX | OKLA | N | 10' | 34-24 | W | 10 | W | +20' |
| 1994 | 5 | SAT | LOU | NCST | H | 2 | 35-14 | W | 21 | W | +23 |
| 1994 | 5 | SAT | RICE | TEX | H | 6' | 19-17 | W | 2 | W | +8' |
| 1995 | 5 | SAT | NCAR | VIR | H | 3' | 22-17 | W | 5 | W | +8' |
| 1996 | 5 | SAT | GEO | TEN | H | 14 | 17-29 | L | -12 | W | +2 |
| 1996 | 5 | SAT | IWST | TXAM | H | 13 | 21-24 | L | -3 | W | +10 |
| 1997 | 5 | SAT | NTX | TXAM | H | 31' | 10-36 | L | -26 | W | +5' |
| 1998 | 5 | SAT | KAN | TXAM | H | 13 | 21-24 | L | -3 | W | +10 |
| 2000 | 5 | SAT | AKR | MIAO | H | 5 | 37-20 | W | 17 | W | +22 |
| 2003 | 5 | SAT | TROY | MRSH | H | 12' | 33-24 | W | 9 | W | +21' |
| 2003 | 5 | SAT | BAY | COLO | H | 19' | 42-30 | W | 12 | W | +31' |
| 2003 | 5 | SAT | TLS | HAW | H | 9 | 27-16 | W | 11 | W | +20 |
| 2005 | 5 | SAT | CFL | MEM | H | 0 | 38-17 | W | 21 | W | +21 |
| 2006 | 5 | SAT | KEST | AKR | H | 1' | 37-15 | W | 22 | W | +23' |

# NCAA FOOTBALL POWER SYSTEM #3

In *Section 3* of the **2008 NCAA FOOTBALL POWER SYSTEM e-CYCLOPEDIA, PRO INFO SPORTS** moves on to investigate how college teams do in the latter half of the season. This featured situation has all the elements of very potent system – a relatively large number of qualifying games, a long history, and a high cover average.

Home favorites struggling through a long season with just a single victory have come up big against opponents also with just one win.

From **Game 8 on,** play **ON** a home favorite of more than 3 points with 1 season SU win off a conference road game vs. an opponent with less than 2 season SU wins.

SU: 19-0 (22.1)     **ATS: 18-0-1 (11.1)**

| YEAR | GM | DAY | TEAM | OPP | ST | LINE | SCORE | SU | MRG | ATS | MRG |
|------|----|-----|------|-----|----|------|-------|----|----|-----|-----|
| 1981 | 8  | SAT | CAL  | ORST | H | -13  | 45-3  | W | 42 | W | +29 |
| 1981 | 8  | SAT | SYR  | CLG  | H | -10  | 47-24 | W | 23 | W | +13 |
| 1981 | 11 | SAT | ORE  | ORST | H | -16' | 47-17 | W | 30 | W | +13' |
| 1985 | 10 | SAT | RUT  | CLG  | H | -8   | 28-14 | W | 14 | W | +6 |
| 1989 | 9  | SAT | PUR  | NORW | H | -7'  | 46-15 | W | 31 | W | +23' |
| 1996 | 8  | SAT | HAW  | UNLV | H | -10  | 38-28 | W | 10 | P | 0 |
| 1996 | 8  | SAT | NCST | DUKE | H | -10  | 44-22 | W | 22 | W | +12 |
| 1996 | 10 | SAT | ORST | NIL  | H | -21  | 67-28 | W | 39 | W | +18 |
| 1997 | 8  | SAT | NMST | AKST | H | -4'  | 34-20 | W | 14 | W | +9' |
| 1997 | 9  | SAT | IND  | ILL  | H | -4'  | 23-3  | W | 20 | W | +15' |
| 1999 | 9  | SAT | KEST | BUF  | H | -14  | 41-20 | W | 21 | W | +7 |
| 1999 | 8  | SAT | TEM  | RUT  | H | -10  | 56-28 | W | 28 | W | +18 |
| 2000 | 8  | SAT | BOWL | EMCH | H | -9'  | 20-6  | W | 14 | W | +4' |
| 2000 | 8  | SAT | SMU  | NEV  | H | -13' | 21-7  | W | 14 | W | +0' |
| 2000 | 9  | SAT | EMCH | CMCH | H | -9   | 31-15 | W | 16 | W | +7 |
| 2000 | 9  | SAT | HAW  | NEV  | H | -14' | 37-17 | W | 20 | W | +5' |
| 2002 | 8  | SAT | SYR  | RUT  | H | -16  | 45-14 | W | 31 | W | +15 |
| 2005 | 10 | SAT | SJST | NMST | H | -8'  | 27-10 | W | 17 | W | +8' |
| 2006 | 9  | SAT | SDST | UNLV | H | -8'  | 21-7  | W | 14 | W | +5' |

# NCAA FOOTBALL POWER SYSTEM #4

In **PRO INFO SPORTS** last look at games that involve certain games of the regular season, *Section 4* of the **NCAA FOOTBALL POWER SYSTEM e-CYCLOPEDIA** reveals some strong situations for season finales. The featured scenario has a very basic set of parameters but has produced more than a dozen winners over the past 20 years.

Teams finishing the season at home and surging on offense over their last 4 games have been unbeatable.

In its **Final Game,** play **ON** a home team off scoring an average of 44+ points in its last 4 games.

SU: 13-0 (28.6)        **ATS: 13-0 (12.4)**

| YEAR | GM | DAY | TEAM | OPP | ST | LINE | SCORE | SU | MRG | ATS | MRG |
|------|----|-----|------|-----|----|----|-------|----|-----|-----|-----|
| 1988 | 11 | SAT | WVA | SYR | H | -7' | 31-9 | W | 22 | W | +14' |
| 1988 | 11 | SAT | FLST | FLA | H | -16' | 52-17 | W | 35 | W | +18' |
| 1990 | 11 | SAT | FLST | FLA | H | -2' | 45-30 | W | 15 | W | +12' |
| 1991 | 12 | SAT | BYU | UTAH | H | -17 | 48-17 | W | 31 | W | +14 |
| 1992 | 11 | SAT | FLST | FLA | H | -17 | 45-24 | W | 21 | W | +4 |
| 1993 | 11 | SAT | BYU | UTEP | H | -21 | 47-16 | W | 31 | W | +10 |
| 1995 | 11 | FRI | NEB | OKLA | H | -34 | 37-0 | W | 37 | W | +3 |
| 1998 | 11 | SAT | LOU | ARMY | H | -8 | 35-23 | W | 12 | W | +4 |
| 1998 | 11 | THU | TLN | LTCH | H | -12 | 63-30 | W | 33 | W | +21 |
| 2001 | 13 | SAT | FRES | UTST | H | -22 | 70-21 | W | 49 | W | +27 |
| 2002 | 12 | SAT | USC | NOTD | H | -11 | 44-13 | W | 31 | W | +20 |
| 2003 | 12 | SAT | USC | ORST | H | -21' | 52-28 | W | 24 | W | +2' |
| 2004 | 11 | SAT | UTAH | BYU | H | -21 | 52-21 | W | 31 | W | +10 |

# NCAA FOOTBALL POWER SYSTEM #5

*Section 5* of the **PRO INFO SPORTS 2008 NCAA FOOTBALL POWER SYSTEM e-CYCLOPEDIA** looks at the good, bad, and ugly college teams. Specifically, we have isolated teams that are either undefeated or winless after various number of games. The situation we feature here reveals a spot in which teams looking for their first win have been absolutely dreadful for nearly 20 years.

After barely failing to get their first victory of the season, disheartened teams have come out flat in their next game.

From **Game 5 on,** play **AGAINST** a winless team (*not* a conference underdog of 12+ points) off a SU loss of less than 3 points.

SU: 16-4 (14.3)      **ATS: 19-0-1 (10.7)**

| YEAR | GM | DAY | TEAM | OPP | ST | LINE | SCORE | SU | MRG | ATS | MRG |
|------|----|-----|------|-----|----|------|-------|----|----|-----|-----|
| 1989 | 5 | SAT | WAKE | NCAR | A | -1' | 17-16 | W | 1 | L | -0' |
| 1989 | 6 | SAT | NORW | WIS | A | 3' | 31-35 | L | -4 | L | -0' |
| 1990 | 6 | SAT | AKST | TOL | A | 7 | 28-43 | L | -15 | L | -8 |
| 1991 | 5 | SAT | NMX | NMST | H | -7 | 17-10 | W | 7 | P | 0 |
| 1991 | 5 | SAT | LLAF | TXAM | A | 25' | 7-34 | L | -27 | L | -1' |
| 1991 | 6 | SAT | KEST | CIN | H | 1 | 19-38 | L | -19 | L | -18 |
| 1991 | 9 | SAT | LLAF | NIL | A | -6 | 13-12 | W | 1 | L | -5 |
| 1991 | 8 | SAT | OKST | KAN | H | 7' | 0-31 | L | -31 | L | -23' |
| 1992 | 8 | SAT | EMCH | OHU | H | -4 | 7-6 | W | 1 | L | -3 |
| 1994 | 5 | SAT | NMX | COST | H | 5 | 31-38 | L | -7 | L | -2 |
| 1994 | 8 | SAT | IWST | MIZ | H | -1' | 20-34 | L | -14 | L | -15' |
| 1995 | 5 | SAT | UTST | COST | H | 18 | 17-59 | L | -42 | L | -24 |
| 1997 | 6 | SAT | TCU | TLS | H | -7' | 22-33 | L | -11 | L | -18' |
| 2000 | 5 | SAT | LLAF | UAB | A | 19 | 2-47 | L | -45 | L | -26 |
| 2000 | 7 | SAT | LLAF | LTCH | A | 6 | 14-48 | L | -34 | L | -28 |
| 2001 | 8 | SAT | NAVY | TLN | H | 2' | 28-42 | L | -14 | L | -11' |
| 2003 | 5 | SAT | MTEN | TEM | H | -3 | 36-44 | L | -8 | L | -11 |
| 2003 | 6 | SAT | SMU | SJST | A | 7' | 14-31 | L | -17 | L | -9' |
| 2004 | 6 | SAT | CFL | AKR | H | -2' | 21-26 | L | -5 | L | -7' |
| 2004 | 10 | SAT | CFL | BALL | A | 3' | 17-21 | L | -4 | L | -0' |

# NCAA FOOTBALL POWER SYSTEM #6

In *Section 6* of the **2008 NCAA FOOTBALL POWER SYSTEM e-CYCLOPEDIA, PRO INFO SPORTS** investigates situations in which favorites have performed consistently. The scenario described below has been perfect for over 2 decades and beat the spread by nearly 2 TDs per contest.

After a loss by the narrowest of margins, heavy favorites have taken no chances on another close call, as they have blistered their opponents while beating the spread for the past 20 seasons.

Play **ON** a Saturday favorite of more than 24 points off a 1-point SU loss scoring less than 34 points vs. an opponent *not* off a non-lined road SU loss.

SU: 13-0 (43.7)      **ATS: 13-0 (13.2)**

| YEAR | GM | DAY | TEAM | OPP | ST | LINE | SCORE | SU | MRG | ATS | MRG |
|------|----|-----|------|-----|----|------|-------|----|-----|-----|-----|
| 1986 | 9 | SAT | AUB | CIN | H | -26 | 52-7 | W | 45 | **W** | **+19** |
| 1988 | 6 | SAT | MIAF | CIN | H | -46 | 57-3 | W | 54 | **W** | **+8** |
| 1989 | 2 | SAT | USC | UTST | H | -48 | 66-10 | W | 56 | **W** | **+8** |
| 1990 | 3 | SAT | STAN | ORST | H | -27 | 37-3 | W | 34 | **W** | **+7** |
| 1990 | 10 | SAT | IOWA | PUR | H | -25' | 38-9 | W | 29 | **W** | **+3'** |
| 1991 | 6 | SAT | TEX | SMU | A | -25 | 34-0 | W | 34 | **W** | **+9** |
| 1993 | 3 | SAT | BCOL | TEM | H | -30' | 66-14 | W | 52 | **W** | **+21'** |
| 2001 | 11 | SAT | NCAR | DUKE | H | -27' | 52-17 | W | 35 | **W** | **+7'** |
| 2004 | 4 | SAT | LSU | MSST | H | -31 | 51-0 | W | 51 | **W** | **+20** |
| 2005 | 2 | SAT | TXAM | SMU | H | -28' | 66-8 | W | 58 | **W** | **+29'** |
| 2005 | 9 | SAT | CLEM | DUKE | H | -28 | 49-20 | W | 29 | **W** | **+1** |
| 2005 | 10 | SAT | GEO | KTKY | H | -24' | 45-13 | W | 32 | **W** | **+7'** |
| 2006 | 4 | SAT | OKLA | MTEN | H | -28' | 59-0 | W | 59 | **W** | **+30'** |

# NCAA FOOTBALL POWER SYSTEM #7

While are often offer tremendous value, the **POWER SYSTEM** below reveals a situation in which dogs have continued to be a "fade" team since at least the early 1980s. This is one of numerous strong underdog scenarios found in *Section 7* of the **PRO INFO SPORTS 2008 NCAA FOOTBALL e-CYCLOPEDIA.**

In the second half of the season, non-conference underdogs have continued to fall after dropping 2 games by more than a FG as conference road dogs.

From **Game 5 on,** play **AGAINST** a non-conference underdog off conference road underdog SU losses of 4+ points in each of its last 2 games.

SU: 15-0 (29.1)      **ATS: 15-0 (11.9)**

| YEAR | GM | DAY | TEAM | OPP | ST | LINE | SCORE | SU | MRG | ATS | MRG |
|------|----|----|----|----|----|----|----|----|----|----|----|
| 1981 | 6 | SAT | VIR | SCAR | A | 12' | 3-21 | L | -18 | L | -5' |
| 1981 | 8 | SAT | KTKY | VTCH | H | 1 | 3-29 | L | -26 | L | -25 |
| 1986 | 6 | SAT | UTAH | AZST | A | 27 | 7-52 | L | -45 | L | -18 |
| 1988 | 8 | SAT | RICE | NOTD | A | 31 | 11-54 | L | -43 | L | -12 |
| 1989 | 5 | SAT | TEM | HOU | A | 43 | 7-65 | L | -58 | L | -15 |
| 1991 | 7 | SAT | ARZ | MIAF | H | 26' | 9-36 | L | -27 | L | -0' |
| 1991 | 10 | SAT | NAVY | WAKE | H | 5' | 24-52 | L | -28 | L | -22' |
| 1996 | 6 | SAT | RUT | ARMY | H | 5 | 21-42 | L | -21 | L | -16 |
| 1996 | 8 | SAT | MEM | LLAF | A | 1' | 9-13 | L | -4 | L | -2' |
| 2001 | 9 | SAT | LMON | TROY | H | 12 | 12-44 | L | -32 | L | -20 |
| 2001 | 12 | SAT | SJST | STAN | H | 19' | 14-41 | L | -27 | L | -7' |
| 2002 | 5 | SAT | TLN | TEX | H | 31' | 0-49 | L | -49 | L | -17' |
| 2003 | 10 | SAT | ARMY | AIR | A | 26' | 3-31 | L | -28 | L | -1' |
| 2004 | 6 | SAT | MSST | UAB | H | 12 | 13-27 | L | -14 | L | -2 |
| 2006 | 6 | SAT | NCAR | SFL | H | 3' | 20-37 | L | -17 | L | -13' |

# NCAA FOOTBALL POWER SYSTEM #8

In *Section 8* of the **PRO INFO SPORTS 2008 NCAA POWER SYSTEM e-CYCLOPEDIA** we turn our attention to college home teams. The **POWER SYSTEM** below has compiled 18 straight spread wins in a little over a decade, covering by more than a dozen points a game.

After losing its 7th game of the year, all hope is lost for a bowl invitation and teams described have come out flat.

Play **AGAINST** a Saturday home team off its 7th SU loss of the season as a favorite of 15 points or less/pick 'em in its last game.

SU: 15-2-1 (19.3)    **ATS: 18-0 (12.3)**

| YEAR | GM | DAY | TEAM | OPP | ST | LINE | SCORE | SU | MRG | ATS | MRG |
|------|----|-----|------|-----|----|------|-------|-----|-----|-----|-----|
| 1994 | 11 | SAT | HAW | MIZ | H | -4 | 32-32 | P | 0 | L | -4 |
| 1996 | 9 | SAT | NIL | LTCH | H | 14' | 14-40 | L | -26 | L | -11' |
| 1996 | 9 | SAT | TEM | MIAF | H | 24 | 26-57 | L | -31 | L | -7 |
| 1997 | 10 | SAT | CMCH | MRSH | H | 23 | 17-45 | L | -28 | L | -5 |
| 1997 | 9 | SAT | LOU | ECAR | H | 2' | 31-45 | L | -14 | L | -11' |
| 1997 | 11 | SAT | HAW | LMON | H | -5' | 20-23 | L | -3 | L | -8' |
| 1998 | 9 | SAT | SCAR | TEN | H | 17 | 14-49 | L | -35 | L | -18 |
| 1999 | 11 | SAT | NEV | UTST | H | -3 | 35-37 | L | -2 | L | -5 |
| 2000 | 8 | SAT | NAVY | TOL | H | 18 | 14-35 | L | -21 | L | -3 |
| 2001 | 10 | SAT | TLN | LOU | H | 11 | 7-52 | L | -45 | L | -34 |
| 2002 | 10 | SAT | WMCH | EMCH | H | -25' | 33-31 | W | 2 | L | -23' |
| 2002 | 11 | SAT | IND | PNST | H | 24 | 25-58 | L | -33 | L | -9 |
| 2002 | 12 | SAT | CMCH | WMCH | H | 2' | 10-35 | L | -25 | L | -22' |
| 2003 | 11 | SAT | UTST | TROY | H | -6' | 14-23 | L | -9 | L | -15' |
| 2003 | 12 | SAT | BALL | BOWL | H | 14' | 14-41 | L | -27 | L | -12' |
| 2004 | 11 | SAT | CMCH | BALL | H | -3' | 41-40 | W | 1 | L | -2' |
| 2005 | 9 | SAT | SYR | SFL | H | 6' | 0-27 | L | -27 | L | -20' |
| 2005 | 10 | SAT | TLN | TLS | H | 15' | 14-38 | L | -24 | L | -8' |

# NCAA FOOTBALL POWER SYSTEM #9

In *Section 9* of the **PRO INFO SPORTS 2008 NCAA FOOTBALL POWER SYSTEM e-CYCLOPEDIA,** we narrow our focus to college home favorites. From that collection we include here a situation that has been perfect for over 20 seasons with 17 consecutive SU & ATS wins, while beating the spread by 2 TDs per game on average.

Following 2 superlative defensive efforts, small home favorites have crushed all the opponents described for 20 seasons.

Play **ON** a home favorite of less than 5 points off allowing less than 8 points in each of its last 2 games vs. an opponent *not* off a conference road favorite SU loss.

SU: 17-0 (16.4)     **ATS: 17-0 (13.6)**

| YEAR | GM | DAY | TEAM | OPP | ST | LINE | SCORE | SU | MRG | ATS | MRG |
|------|----|-----|------|-----|----|----|-------|----|----|----|----|
| 1985 | 9 | SAT | OKLA | NEB | H | -3 | 27-7 | W | 20 | W | +17 |
| 1985 | 11 | THU | TXAM | TEX | H | -4' | 42-10 | W | 32 | W | +27' |
| 1987 | 3 | SAT | UTEP | HAW | H | -3' | 37-13 | W | 24 | W | +20' |
| 1988 | 5 | SAT | FLA | LSU | H | -0' | 19-6 | W | 13 | W | +12' |
| 1989 | 11 | SAT | MIAF | NOTD | H | -1' | 27-10 | W | 17 | W | +15' |
| 1991 | 7 | SAT | ALA | TEN | H | -2 | 24-19 | W | 5 | W | +3 |
| 1991 | 11 | SAT | PNST | NOTD | H | -3' | 35-13 | W | 22 | W | +18' |
| 1993 | 4 | SAT | MIS | GEO | H | -3 | 31-14 | W | 17 | W | +14 |
| 1994 | 7 | SAT | VIR | NCAR | H | -3 | 34-10 | W | 24 | W | +21 |
| 1995 | 9 | SAT | CLEM | NCAR | H | -2 | 17-10 | W | 7 | W | +5 |
| 1997 | 3 | SAT | FLA | TEN | H | -4 | 33-20 | W | 13 | W | +9 |
| 1998 | 9 | SAT | ARZ | ORE | H | -2' | 38-3 | W | 35 | W | +32' |
| 1999 | 11 | SAT | MCST | PNST | H | -2 | 35-28 | W | 7 | W | +5 |
| 2003 | 5 | SAT | AUB | TEN | H | -1 | 28-21 | W | 7 | W | +6 |
| 2004 | 4 | SAT | WIS | PNST | H | -3 | 16-3 | W | 13 | W | +10 |
| 2004 | 4 | SAT | TXAM | KAST | H | -4 | 42-30 | W | 12 | W | +8 |
| 2005 | 9 | SAT | VIR | GTCH | H | -3 | 27-17 | W | 10 | W | +7 |

# NCAA FOOTBALL POWER SYSTEM #10

*Section 10* of the **2008 NCAA FOOTBALL POWER SYSTEM e-CYCLOPEDIA** deals exclusively with college home underdogs. **PRO INFO SPORTS** features such a situation here that has an unblemished record after 20 seasons.

After a razor-close victory as a home underdog, teams back in the home dog role have used the momentum for another strong performance.

Play **ON** a home underdog of less than 28 points off a home underdog SU win of less than 3 points.

SU: 9-6 (0.5)        **ATS: 15-0 (9.3)**

| YEAR | GM | DAY | TEAM | OPP | ST | LINE | SCORE | SU | MRG | ATS | MRG |
|------|----|----|------|-----|----|------|-------|----|----|----|----|
| 1988 | 12 | SAT | NMX | SDST | H | +13' | 10-18 | L | -8 | W | +5' |
| 1989 | 10 | SAT | CAL | WAST | H | +10' | 38-26 | W | 12 | W | +22' |
| 1991 | 5 | SAT | TLS | MIAF | H | +27 | 10-34 | L | -24 | W | +3 |
| 1991 | 8 | SAT | ARK | BAY | H | +7 | 5-9 | L | -4 | W | +3 |
| 1992 | 7 | SAT | OKST | IWST | H | +3' | 27-21 | W | 6 | W | +9' |
| 1992 | 10 | SAT | CIN | KTKY | H | +2' | 17-13 | W | 4 | W | +6' |
| 1993 | 4 | SAT | LLAF | SMIS | H | +9 | 13-7 | W | 6 | W | +15 |
| 1998 | 4 | SAT | NMST | UTEP | H | +7 | 33-24 | W | 9 | W | +16 |
| 1998 | 8 | SAT | MIN | MICH | H | +12' | 10-15 | L | -5 | W | +7' |
| 2000 | 8 | SAT | STAN | WAS | H | +7 | 28-31 | L | -3 | W | +4 |
| 2001 | 11 | SAT | VIR | VTCH | H | +15 | 17-31 | L | -14 | W | +1 |
| 2003 | 9 | SAT | LLAF | IDA | H | +3 | 31-20 | W | 11 | W | +14 |
| 2006 | 4 | SAT | WAS | UCLA | H | +3 | 29-19 | W | 10 | W | +13 |
| 2006 | 5 | THU | NCST | FLST | H | +9' | 24-20 | W | 4 | W | +13' |
| 2006 | 12 | SAT | RICE | SMU | H | +1 | 31-27 | W | 4 | W | +5 |

# NCAA FOOTBALL POWER SYSTEM #11

Turning our attention to the road, *Section 11* of the **PRO INFO SPORTS 2008 NCAA FOOTBALL e-CYCLOPEDIA** looks at how teams do in various situations as visitors. This featured **POWER SYSTEM** has not lost in 15 qualifying games since 1990, beating the spread by more than a dozen ppg on average.

Despite being offensively impotent in their last 2 games, conference road teams have been quite competitive under the conditions outlined.

In **Games 3-10,** play **ON** a conference road team (*not* an underdog of 47+ points) off 2 SU losses scoring less than 4 points in each game vs. an opponent not off a conference road underdog SU & ATS loss.

SU: 7-8 (-3.9)        **ATS: 14-0-1 (12.3)**

| YEAR | GM | DAY | TEAM | OPP | ST | LINE | SCORE | SU | MRG | ATS | MRG |
|------|----|-----|------|-----|----|------|-------|----|----|-----|-----|
| 1990 | 7 | SAT | PUR | MCST | A | 24' | 33-55 | L | -22 | **W** | **+2'** |
| 1992 | 6 | SAT | OHU | BOWL | A | 18 | 14-31 | L | -17 | **W** | **+1** |
| 1995 | 9 | SAT | MARY | NCST | A | 6 | 30-13 | W | 17 | **W** | **+23** |
| 1998 | 5 | SAT | HAW | SDST | A | 22 | 13-35 | L | -22 | **P** | **0** |
| 2000 | 5 | SAT | SDST | WYO | A | 3' | 34-0 | W | 34 | **W** | **+37'** |
| 2000 | 8 | SAT | BAY | TEX | A | 41 | 14-48 | L | -34 | **W** | **+7** |
| 2001 | 10 | SAT | OHU | MRSH | A | 24' | 18-42 | L | -24 | **W** | **+0'** |
| 2001 | 10 | SAT | TEM | WVA | A | 16' | 17-14 | W | 3 | **W** | **+19'** |
| 2002 | 10 | SAT | UTEP | NEV | A | 27' | 17-23 | L | -6 | **W** | **+21'** |
| 2003 | 3 | SAT | AUB | VAN | A | -12 | 45-7 | W | 38 | **W** | **+26** |
| 2003 | 6 | SAT | ARMY | LOU | A | 31 | 10-34 | L | -24 | **W** | **+7** |
| 2003 | 9 | SAT | AKST | NMST | A | 15 | 28-24 | W | 4 | **W** | **+19** |
| 2005 | 4 | SAT | BUF | WMCH | A | 11 | 21-31 | L | -10 | **W** | **+1** |
| 2005 | 5 | SAT | BALL | WMCH | A | 11' | 60-57 | W | 3 | **W** | **+14'** |
| 2006 | 10 | SAT | PUR | MCST | A | 2 | 17-15 | W | 2 | **W** | **+4** |

# NCAA FOOTBALL POWER SYSTEM #12

*Section 12* of the **PRO INFO SPORTS 2008 NCAA FOOTBALL POWER SYSTEM e-CYCLOPEDIA** investigates some strong situations involving road favorites. The selected scenario below has been outstanding since the early 1980s, crushing the spread by more than 15 ppg on average.

Teams with winning records have continued to stumble as road favorites after dropping 2 games in which they were also favored.

In **Games 3-10,** play **AGAINST** a +.500% road favorite of 19 points or less off 2 favorite SU losses vs. an opponent *not* off a SU loss of 24+ points.

SU: 11-3 (8.1)          **ATS: 14-0 (15.5)**

| YEAR | GM | DAY | TEAM | OPP | ST | LINE | SCORE | SU | MRG | ATS | MRG |
|------|----|----|------|------|----|------|-------|----|----|-----|-----|
| 1983 | 8 | SAT | AZST | CAL | A | -8' | 24-26 | L | -2 | **L** | **-10'** |
| 1983 | 10 | SAT | NCAR | VIR | A | -15' | 14-17 | L | -3 | **L** | **-18'** |
| 1989 | 10 | SAT | WAST | CAL | A | -10' | 26-38 | L | -12 | **L** | **-22'** |
| 1991 | 10 | SAT | MIAO | WMCH | A | -2' | 23-24 | L | -1 | **L** | **-3'** |
| 1996 | 10 | SAT | AIR | FRES | A | -10 | 44-38 | W | 6 | **L** | **-4** |
| 1997 | 10 | SAT | AIR | HAW | A | -11 | 34-27 | W | 7 | **L** | **-4** |
| 1999 | 8 | SAT | MICH | IND | A | -16' | 34-31 | W | 3 | **L** | **-13'** |
| 2001 | 10 | SAT | UCLA | USC | A | -3' | 0-27 | L | -27 | **L** | **-30'** |
| 2001 | 10 | THU | MIS | MSST | A | -3 | 28-36 | L | -8 | **L** | **-11** |
| 2003 | 7 | SAT | ORE | AZST | A | -2' | 14-59 | L | -45 | **L** | **-47'** |
| 2004 | 6 | SAT | OHST | IOWA | A | -1 | 7-33 | L | -26 | **L** | **-27** |
| 2004 | 8 | SAT | PUR | NORW | A | -10 | 10-13 | L | -3 | **L** | **-13** |
| 2004 | 9 | SAT | PUR | IOWA | A | -1 | 21-23 | L | -2 | **L** | **-3** |
| 2006 | 10 | SAT | PIT | CIN | A | -7' | 45-46 | L | -1 | **L** | **-8'** |

# NCAA FOOTBALL POWER SYSTEM #13

**PRO INFO SPORTS** reveals some strong **POWER SYSTEMS** involving road favorites in *Section 13* of the **2008 NCAA FOOTBALL e-CYCLOPEDIA.** This situation featured here has not suffered a loss in 18 qualifying games going back to at least 1980, and picked up another win last season.

After losing a game as a double-digit road favorite, teams have responded strongly as a road underdog of more than 5 points.

Play **ON** a road underdog or more than 5 points off a non-conference road/neutral SU loss as a favorite of 10+ points.

SU: 7-10-1 (0.3)          **ATS: 17-0-1 (10.5)**

| YEAR | GM | DAY | TEAM | OPP | ST | LINE | SCORE | SU | MRG | ATS | MRG |
|------|----|-----|------|-----|----|------|-------|----|----|-----|-----|
| 1980 | 5 | SAT | LSU | FLA | A | 6' | 24-7 | W | 17 | W | +23' |
| 1980 | 9 | SAT | NOTD | ALA | A | 7 | 7-0 | W | 7 | W | +14 |
| 1982 | 11 | SAT | NOTD | USC | A | 10 | 13-17 | L | -4 | W | +6 |
| 1985 | 9 | SAT | SMIS | ALA | A | 15 | 13-24 | L | -11 | W | +4 |
| 1987 | 3 | SAT | NMX | ARZ | A | 23 | 9-20 | L | -11 | W | +12 |
| 1990 | 3 | SAT | SJST | STAN | A | 8' | 29-23 | W | 6 | W | +14' |
| 1992 | 3 | THU | CAL | KAN | A | 6' | 27-23 | W | 4 | W | +10' |
| 1992 | 6 | SAT | OKLA | COLO | A | 6' | 24-24 | P | 0 | W | +6' |
| 1994 | 2 | SAT | NCST | CLEM | A | 7 | 29-12 | W | 17 | W | +24 |
| 1995 | 3 | SAT | ORST | AZST | A | 9 | 11-20 | L | -9 | P | 0 |
| 1996 | 2 | SAT | UTAH | STAN | A | 6 | 17-10 | W | 7 | W | +13 |
| 1998 | 4 | SAT | ARMY | ECAR | A | 13 | 25-30 | L | -5 | W | +8 |
| 1999 | 5 | SAT | MIAF | FLST | A | 14 | 21-31 | L | -10 | W | +4 |
| 2002 | 4 | SAT | BYU | GTCH | A | 9' | 19-28 | L | -9 | W | +0' |
| 2003 | 3 | SAT | UNLV | WIS | A | 20 | 23-5 | W | 18 | W | +38 |
| 2005 | 3 | SAT | PIT | NEB | A | 8 | 6-7 | L | -1 | W | +7 |
| 2006 | 10 | SAT | BOWL | AKR | A | +7' | 28-35 | L | -7 | W | +0' |
| *2007* | *4* | *SAT* | *IOWA* | *WIS* | *A* | *+7* | *13-17* | *L* | *-4* | *W* | *+3* |

# NCAA FOOTBALL POWER SYSTEM #14

Non-Saturday college games are the NCAA version of the NFL's Sunday Night and Monday Night games and have become quite popular in recent seasons. Just as we do with the pros, **PRO INFO SPORTS** isolates how college teams do in relation to these highlighted contests. In *Section 14* of the **2008 NCAA FOOTBALL POWER SYSTEM e-CYCLOPEDIA,** we examine how teams perform *before* and *after* non-Saturday games and feature one here that has had an amazing 21 straight victories just since 2000, including 3 wins last year.

With a mid-week game coming up, home teams have been rock solid under the right conditions, as described.

Play **ON** a home team (*not* a favorite of 24+ points) before 6+ days rest and a Tuesday/Wednesday road contest and *not* off a road favorite SU loss vs. an opponent *not* off a SU loss of 41+ points.

SU: 18-3 (17.8)     **ATS: 21-0 (13.3)**

| YEAR | GM | DAY | TEAM | OPP | ST | LINE | SCORE | SU | MRG | ATS | MRG |
|------|----|-----|------|-----|----|------|-------|----|----|-----|-----|
| 2000 | 10 | SAT | BOWL | OHU | H | +9 | 21-23 | L | -2 | W | +7 |
| 2001 | 7 | SAT | ECAR | MEM | H | -10 | 32-11 | W | 21 | W | +11 |
| 2002 | 5 | THU | LOU | FLST | H | +14' | 26-20 | W | 6 | W | +20' |
| 2002 | 10 | SAT | MIAO | OHU | H | -16' | 38-20 | W | 18 | W | +1' |
| 2002 | 10 | SAT | WVA | BCOL | H | -3' | 24-14 | W | 10 | W | +6' |
| 2003 | 4 | SAT | HOU | MSST | H | +4' | 42-35 | W | 7 | W | +11' |
| 2003 | 6 | SAT | VTCH | SYR | H | -17' | 51-7 | W | 44 | W | +26' |
| 2003 | 9 | SAT | MRSH | AKR | H | -14 | 42-24 | W | 18 | W | +4 |
| 2003 | 11 | SAT | NTX | AKST | H | -21 | 58-14 | W | 44 | W | +23 |
| 2004 | 10 | SAT | BOWL | MRSH | H | -10 | 56-35 | W | 21 | W | +11 |
| 2004 | 10 | SAT | KEST | EMCH | H | -12' | 69-17 | W | 52 | W | +39' |
| 2005 | 4 | WED | MIAO | CIN | H | -10 | 44-16 | W | 28 | W | +18 |
| 2005 | 8 | WED | WVA | CON | H | -15 | 45-13 | W | 32 | W | +17 |
| 2005 | 9 | FRI | OHU | TOL | H | +11 | 21-30 | L | -9 | W | +2 |
| 2005 | 10 | SAT | WMCH | CMCH | H | -2 | 31-24 | W | 7 | W | +5 |
| 2006 | 3 | SAT | SMIS | NCST | H | -3 | 37-17 | W | 20 | W | +17 |
| 2006 | 4 | TUE | CFL | SMIS | H | +6 | 14-19 | L | -5 | W | +1 |
| 2006 | 9 | SAT | TOL | AKR | H | +3' | 35-20 | W | 15 | W | +18' |
| 2007 | 5 | SAT | NAVY | AIR | H | -2' | 31-20 | W | 11 | W | +8' |
| 2007 | 10 | SAT | TOL | EMCH | H | -8 | 52-28 | W | 24 | W | +16 |
| 2007 | 10 | WED | AKR | OHU | H | +3 | 48-37 | W | 11 | W | +14 |

# NCAA FOOTBALL POWER SYSTEM #15

Continuing with our focus on non-Saturday games, *Section 15* of the **PRO INFO SPORTS 2008 NCAA FOOTBALL POWER SYSTEM e-CYCLOPEDIA** looks at how teams do in these primetime pairings under various conditions. The situation described below has been strong since 1995, blasting the spread by nearly 15 ppg on average.

After 2 offensive explosions, non-Saturday home teams have kept rolling under the conditions described.

Play **ON** a non-Saturday home team off an ATS win scoring 39+ points in its last game and scoring 39+ points before that and *not* before a non-Saturday conference road game.

SU: 15-0 (26.7)     **ATS: 13-0-2 (14.9)**

| YEAR | GM | DAY | TEAM | OPP | ST | LINE | SCORE | SU | MRG | ATS | MRG |
|------|----|-----|------|-----|----|------|-------|----|----|-----|-----|
| 1995 | 11 | FRI | NEB | OKLA | H | -34 | 37-0 | W | 37 | **W** | +3 |
| 1998 | 11 | THU | TLN | LTCH | H | -12 | 63-30 | W | 33 | **W** | +21 |
| 1999 | 11 | FRI | VTCH | BCOL | H | -24 | 38-14 | W | 24 | **P** | 0 |
| 1999 | 13 | THU | BOIS | LOU | H | 1' | 34-31 | W | 3 | **W** | +4' |
| 2000 | 4 | THU | NCST | GTCH | H | -3 | 30-23 | W | 7 | **W** | +4 |
| 2000 | 12 | THU | BOIS | UTEP | H | -9 | 38-23 | W | 15 | **W** | +6 |
| 2001 | 9 | THU | BYU | COST | H | -14' | 56-34 | W | 22 | **W** | +7' |
| 2001 | 12 | FRI | HAW | BYU | H | 3 | 72-45 | W | 27 | **W** | +30 |
| 2002 | 7 | FRI | BOIS | FRES | H | -7 | 67-21 | W | 46 | **W** | +39 |
| 2002 | 8 | WED | TCU | SMIS | H | -2' | 37-7 | W | 30 | **W** | +27' |
| 2003 | 12 | FRI | BOWL | TOL | H | -8 | 31-23 | W | 8 | **P** | 0 |
| 2004 | 9 | FRI | FRES | HAW | H | -21 | 70-14 | W | 56 | **W** | +35 |
| 2004 | 13 | FRI | HAW | UAB | H | -4 | 59-40 | W | 19 | **W** | +15 |
| 2005 | 8 | THU | LOU | PIT | H | -21 | 42-20 | W | 22 | **W** | +1 |
| 2005 | 9 | FRI | LOU | RUT | H | -21' | 56-5 | W | 51 | **W** | +29' |

# NCAA FOOTBALL POWER SYSTEM #16

*Revenge* is a college football situation in which teams have performed consistently under certain conditions. *Section 16* of the **PRO INFO SPORTS 2008 NCAA FOOTBALL e-CYCLOPEDIA** deals with such scenarios, including the **POWER SYSTEM** offered below that has been in effect for over 20 years, blowing up the spread by more than 16 ppg on average.

Despite playing without rest, home underdogs looking to avenge a home dog loss last year in which they actually beat the spread by more than a FG, have been very competitive.

Play **ON** a home underdog with less than 7 days rest seeking revenge for a home underdog SU loss and ATS win of more than 3 points in the previous matchup last season and *not* off a shutout SU loss in its last game.

SU: 7-8 (3.8)          **ATS: 14-0-1 (16.3)**

| YEAR | GM | DAY | TEAM | OPP | ST | LINE | SCORE | SU | MRG | ATS | MRG |
|------|----|-----|------|-----|----|------|-------|----|-----|-----|-----|
| 1987 | 9 | SAT | WIS | OHST | H | 18' | 26-24 | W | 2 | **W** | **+20'** |
| 1989 | 7 | SAT | HAW | BYU | H | 3' | 56-14 | W | 42 | **W** | **+45'** |
| 1989 | 12 | SAT | UTAH | AIR | H | 22 | 38-42 | L | -4 | **W** | **+18** |
| 1992 | 2 | SAT | ORST | FRES | H | 12' | 46-36 | W | 10 | **W** | **+22'** |
| 1993 | 11 | SAT | TEM | PIT | H | 20 | 18-28 | L | -10 | **W** | **+10** |
| 1994 | 2 | SAT | MARY | FLST | H | 33' | 20-52 | L | -32 | **W** | **+1'** |
| 1995 | 9 | SAT | CAL | WAST | H | 3 | 27-11 | W | 16 | **W** | **+19** |
| 1995 | 10 | SAT | KEST | BOWL | H | 13' | 15-26 | L | -11 | **W** | **+2'** |
| 1996 | 5 | SAT | UTEP | UTAH | H | 17 | 27-34 | L | -7 | **W** | **+10** |
| 1997 | 3 | SAT | ORST | AZST | H | 11 | 10-13 | L | -3 | **W** | **+8** |
| 1997 | 7 | SAT | KEST | CMCH | H | 2' | 60-37 | W | 23 | **W** | **+25'** |
| 1999 | 7 | SAT | ORST | UCLA | H | 1 | 55-7 | W | 48 | **W** | **+49** |
| 2002 | 9 | SAT | VAN | ALA | H | 22 | 8-30 | L | -22 | **P** | **0** |
| 2002 | 10 | SAT | KTKY | LSU | H | 5 | 30-33 | L | -3 | **W** | **+2** |
| 2003 | 12 | SAT | HAW | ALA | H | 2' | 37-29 | W | 8 | **W** | **+10'** |

# NCAA FOOTBALL POWER SYSTEM #17

In *Section 17* of the **2008 NCAA FOOTBALL e-CYCLOPEDIA, PRO INFO SPORTS** examines various situations involving teams coming off a shutout, both as victor and vanquished. The featured **POWER SYSTEM** below has been perfect since at least 1981, while managing an average spread cover of more than a dozen points.

Without a 3-game road trip staring them in the fact, teams off a home favorite shutout win and now favored at home by just 3 points or less, have had little problem disposing of visitors.

Play **ON** a home favorite of 3 points or less off a home favorite shutout SU win and *not* before 3 road games.

SU: 15-0 (14.1)          **ATS: 15-0 (12.1)**

| YEAR | GM | DAY | TEAM | OPP | ST | LINE | SCORE | SU | MRG | ATS | MRG |
|------|----|-----|------|-----|----|------|-------|----|----|-----|-----|
| 1981 | 10 | SAT | UCLA | AZST | H | -1 | 34-24 | W | 10 | W | +9 |
| 1983 | 4 | SAT | MIAF | NOTD | H | -0' | 20-0 | W | 20 | W | +19' |
| 1984 | 3 | SAT | OHST | IOWA | H | -3 | 45-26 | W | 19 | W | +16 |
| 1985 | 9 | SAT | OKLA | NEB | H | -3 | 27-7 | W | 20 | W | +17 |
| 1987 | 2 | SAT | KTKY | IND | H | -1 | 34-15 | W | 19 | W | +18 |
| 1988 | 4 | SAT | SCAR | GEO | H | -2 | 23-10 | W | 13 | W | +11 |
| 1988 | 5 | SAT | FLA | LSU | H | -0' | 19-6 | W | 13 | W | +12' |
| 1991 | 7 | SAT | ALA | TEN | H | -2 | 24-19 | W | 5 | W | +3 |
| 1992 | 9 | SAT | MIS | MEM | H | -2 | 17-12 | W | 5 | W | +3 |
| 1994 | 5 | SAT | CAL | UCLA | H | -3 | 26-7 | W | 19 | W | +16 |
| 1996 | 4 | SAT | WYO | AIR | H | -2 | 22-19 | W | 3 | W | +1 |
| 1999 | 8 | SAT | WIS | MCST | H | -2 | 40-10 | W | 30 | W | +28 |
| 2000 | 4 | THU | NCST | GTCH | H | -3 | 30-23 | W | 7 | W | +4 |
| 2003 | 9 | SAT | UTST | MTEN | H | -2 | 41-20 | W | 21 | W | +19 |
| 2006 | 9 | SAT | VIR | NCST | H | -2 | 14-7 | W | 7 | W | +5 |

# NCAA FOOTBALL POWER SYSTEM #18

*Overtime* is a relatively recent phenomena that has been introduced into college football. Nonetheless, some strong patterns have already emerged that we document in *Section 18* of the **PRO INFO SPORTS 2008 NCAA FOOTBALL POWER SYSTEM e-CYCLOPEDIA.** The situation we reveal here has a few basic parameters, but has already managed a run of 21 consecutive wins in a row just since 1999.

After an OT win, road teams favored by more than FG have stumbled under the conditions outlined.

Play **AGAINST** road favorite of more than 3 points off an OT SU win scoring 17+ points as a favorite of 22 points or less.

SU: 12-9 (3.4)          **ATS: 21-0 (12.3)**

| YEAR | GM | DAY | TEAM | OPP | ST | LINE | SCORE | SU | MRG | ATS | MRG |
|------|----|----|------|------|----|------|-------|----|----|----|----|
| 1999 | 6 | SAT | GTCH | DUKE | A | -16' | 38-31 | W | 7 | L | -9' |
| 1999 | 6 | SAT | COLO | TXT | A | -5 | 10-31 | L | -21 | L | -26 |
| 1999 | 9 | SAT | FRES | TLS | A | -14' | 28-14 | W | 14 | L | -0' |
| 2000 | 9 | SAT | ORE | WAST | A | -9' | 27-24 | W | 3 | L | -6' |
| 2000 | 10 | SAT | SMIS | CIN | A | -5 | 24-27 | L | -3 | L | -8 |
| 2002 | 7 | SAT | MICH | PUR | A | -3' | 23-21 | W | 2 | L | -1' |
| 2003 | 5 | SAT | MIZ | KAN | A | -9' | 14-35 | L | -21 | L | -30' |
| 2003 | 6 | SAT | NIL | CMCH | A | -17' | 40-24 | W | 16 | L | -1' |
| 2003 | 9 | SAT | SFL | ECAR | A | -11 | 38-37 | W | 1 | L | -10 |
| 2004 | 4 | SAT | MIS | WYO | A | -3' | 32-37 | L | -5 | L | -8' |
| 2004 | 5 | SAT | NCST | NCAR | A | -10' | 24-30 | L | -6 | L | -16' |
| 2004 | 8 | SAT | TXAM | BAY | A | -25 | 34-35 | L | -1 | L | -26 |
| 2004 | 10 | SAT | SYR | TEM | A | -8 | 24-34 | L | -10 | L | -18 |
| 2004 | 12 | SAT | NORW | HAW | A | -6 | 41-49 | L | -8 | L | -14 |
| 2005 | 9 | SAT | UCLA | ARZ | A | -8 | 14-52 | L | -38 | L | -46 |
| 2005 | 9 | SAT | LLAF | NTX | A | -4 | 31-28 | W | 3 | L | -1 |
| 2005 | 10 | SAT | FLA | SCAR | A | -5' | 22-30 | L | -8 | L | -13' |
| 2005 | 10 | SAT | ORE | WAST | A | -3' | 34-31 | W | 3 | L | -0' |
| 2006 | 4 | SAT | BCOL | NCST | A | -6' | 15-17 | L | -2 | L | -8' |
| 2007 | 3 | SAT | MIN | FATL | A | -7 | 39-42 | L | -3 | L | -10 |
| 2007 | 5 | SAT | WAKE | DUKE | A | -7' | 41-36 | W | 5 | L | -2' |

# NCAA FOOTBALL POWER SYSTEM #19

*Section 19* of the **PRO INFO SPORTS 2008 NCAA FOOTBALL e-CYCLOPEDIA** contains our collection of **POWER SYSTEMS** that deal with how teams do before and after unusual breaks between games. Whether it be fewer days that a whole week off or an extended break, some strong situations have been uncovered, such as the one offered below that has been perfect since at least 1981.

Instead of being rusty, very-well rested teams have been ready for a big outing as a road favorite.

Play **ON** a road favorite with 19+ days rest vs. an opponent *not* off a non-conference road underdog SU loss.

SU: 11-0 (26.4)      **ATS: 11-0 (14.4)**

| YEAR | GM | DAY | TEAM | OPP | ST | LINE | SCORE | SU | MRG | ATS | MRG |
|------|----|-----|------|-----|----|------|-------|----|----|-----|-----|
| 1981 | 11 | SAT | GEO | GTCH | A | -22 | 44-7 | W | 37 | W | +15 |
| 1985 | 2 | SAT | SMU | TCU | A | -10' | 56-21 | W | 35 | W | +24' |
| 1987 | 2 | SAT | MIAF | ARK | A | -5' | 51-7 | W | 44 | W | +38' |
| 1989 | 2 | SAT | HOU | AZST | A | -9 | 36-7 | W | 29 | W | +20 |
| 1990 | 6 | SUN | SJST | NMST | A | -35 | 56-20 | W | 36 | W | +1 |
| 1991 | 6 | SAT | DUKE | MARY | A | -1 | 17-13 | W | 4 | W | +3 |
| 1997 | 8 | SAT | IDA | NMST | A | -10' | 35-18 | W | 17 | W | +6' |
| 2001 | 3 | SAT | MIS | KTKY | A | -8 | 42-31 | W | 11 | W | +3 |
| 2003 | 3 | SAT | SFL | ARMY | A | -19 | 28-0 | W | 28 | W | +9 |
| 2004 | 3 | SAT | CAL | ORST | A | -7 | 49-7 | W | 42 | W | +35 |
| 2005 | 3 | SAT | NAVY | DUKE | A | -4 | 28-21 | W | 7 | W | +3 |

# NCAA FOOTBALL POWER SYSTEM #20

**PRO INFO SPORTS** has uncovered so many **POWER SYSTEMS** involving how colleges do either *before* or *after* playing certain opponents, that we had to break it down into 4 sections. *Section 20* of the **2008 NCAA FOOTBALL e-CYCLOPEDIA** looks at how teams do *before* playing college foes *A-M.* Here a situation is revealed that has been perfect for 20 seasons.

Small home favorites have floundered before playing Mississippi.

Play **AGAINST** a home favorite of 1½-6½ points before playing **Mississippi**

SU: 11-3-2 (6.2)      **ATS: 16-0 (10.2)**

| YEAR | GM | DAY | TEAM | OPP | ST | LINE | SCORE | SU | MRG | ATS | MRG |
|------|----|-----|------|-----|----|----|-------|----|----|-----|-----|
| 1988 | 8 | SAT | TEN | BCOL | H | -4 | 10-7 | W | 4 | L | -1 |
| 1989 | 7 | SAT | LSU | TEN | H | -2 | 39-45 | L | -6 | L | -8 |
| 1990 | 1 | SAT | MEM | AKST | H | -3 | 24-24 | T | 0 | L | -3 |
| 1990 | 9 | SAT | TEN | NOTD | H | -3' | 29-34 | L | -5 | L | -8' |
| 1993 | 6 | SAT | ALA | TEN | H | -5 | 17-17 | T | 0 | L | -5 |
| 1995 | 8 | SAT | MEM | TLS | H | -5' | 10-7 | W | 3 | L | -2' |
| 1996 | 3 | SAT | TEN | FLA | H | -3 | 29-35 | L | -6 | L | -9 |
| 1996 | 8 | SAT | LSU | ALA | H | -3 | 0-26 | L | -26 | L | -29 |
| 1996 | 10 | SAT | MSST | ARK | H | -6 | 13-16 | L | -3 | L | -9 |
| 1997 | 9 | SAT | GEO | AUB | H | -5' | 34-45 | L | -11 | L | -16' |
| 1998 | 4 | SAT | SCAR | MSST | H | -2' | 0-38 | L | -38 | L | -40' |
| 2000 | 9 | SAT | LSU | ALA | H | -3 | 30-28 | W | 2 | L | -1 |
| 2002 | 6 | SAT | ALA | GEO | H | -4' | 25-27 | L | -2 | L | -6' |
| 2003 | 6 | SAT | ARK | FLA | H | -4' | 28-33 | L | -5 | L | -9' |
| 2005 | 8 | SAT | ARK | SCAR | H | -6 | 10-14 | L | -4 | L | -10 |
| 2007 | 6 | SAT | ARK | AUB | H | -2' | 7-9 | L | -2 | L | -4' |

# NCAA FOOTBALL POWER SYSTEM #21

*Section 21* of the **PRO INFO SPORTS 2008 NCAA FOOTBALL POWER SYSTEM e-CYCLOPEDIA** continues our examination of how teams do *before* facing certain opponents *(N-Z)*. The situation featured here has a relatively small sample of a dozen qualifying games, but is included because of an amazing average spread cover of 3 TDs, including 2 easy wins last season.

Home favorites of more than a FG have been able to completely focus on the business at hand with a game at Rice on deck and not off a non-lined home victory.

Play **AGAINST** a home favorite of more than 3 points before playing at **Rice** and *not* off a non-lined home SU win.

SU: 6-6 (8.2)         **ATS: 12-0 (21.2)**

| YEAR | GM | DAY | TEAM | OPP | ST | LINE | SCORE | SU | MRG | ATS | MRG |
|------|----|----|------|------|----|------|-------|----|-----|-----|-----|
| 1983 | 1 | SAT | LSU | FLST | H | -5 | 35-40 | L | -5 | L | -10 |
| 1988 | 4 | SAT | TEX | NTX | H | -18 | 27-24 | W | 3 | L | -15 |
| 1992 | 9 | SAT | BAY | GTCH | H | -6' | 31-27 | W | 4 | L | -2' |
| 1997 | 1 | SAT | AIR | IDA | H | -17 | 14-10 | W | 4 | L | -13 |
| 1997 | 2 | SAT | TEX | UCLA | H | -10 | 3-66 | L | -63 | L | -73 |
| 1997 | 4 | FRI | BYU | UTST | H | -14' | 42-35 | W | 7 | L | -7' |
| 1998 | 2 | SAT | NORW | DUKE | H | -12' | 10-44 | L | -34 | L | -46' |
| 2003 | 2 | SAT | TEX | ARK | H | -13' | 28-38 | L | -10 | L | -23' |
| 2004 | 1 | SAT | HAW | FATL | H | -21 | 28-35 | L | -7 | L | -28 |
| 2005 | 5 | SAT | NAVY | KEST | H | -11' | 34-31 | W | 3 | L | -8' |
| 2007 | 2 | SAT | TXT | UTEP | H | -24 | 45-31 | W | 14 | L | -10 |
| 2007 | 6 | SAT | MEM | MTEN | H | -3' | 7-21 | L | -14 | L | -17' |

# NCAA FOOTBALL POWER SYSTEM #22

Just as patterns exist as to how teams react before taking on certain opponents, we document how colleges do *after* playing specified foes. *Section 22* of the **PRO INFO SPORTS 2008 NCAA FOOTBALL POWER SYSTEM e-CYCLOPEDIA** begins this examination with college teams *A-M*.

After falling to Mississippi State, home underdogs have played with no confidence.

Play **AGAINST** a home underdog off a SU loss to **Mississippi St**.

SU: 12-0 (19.4)    **ATS: 12-0 (11.0)**

| YEAR | GM | DAY | TEAM | OPP | ST | LINE | SCORE | SU | MRG | ATS | MRG |
|------|----|----|------|-----|----|------|-------|----|----|-----|-----|
| 1989 | 8 | SAT | MEM | SMIS | H | 6 | 7-31 | L | -24 | L | -18 |
| 1991 | 4 | SAT | TLN | RICE | H | 7' | 19-28 | L | -9 | L | -1' |
| 1991 | 6 | SAT | KTKY | LSU | H | 2 | 26-29 | L | -3 | L | -1 |
| 1991 | 8 | SAT | AUB | FLA | H | 9' | 10-31 | L | -21 | L | -11' |
| 1994 | 9 | SAT | KTKY | VAN | H | 2' | 6-24 | L | -18 | L | -15' |
| 1997 | 5 | SAT | SCAR | AUB | H | 7' | 6-23 | L | -17 | L | -9' |
| 1999 | 5 | SAT | SCAR | MIS | H | 6' | 10-36 | L | -26 | L | -19' |
| 1999 | 7 | SAT | AUB | FLA | H | 16 | 14-32 | L | -18 | L | -2 |
| 1999 | 8 | SAT | LSU | MIS | H | 4' | 23-42 | L | -19 | L | -14' |
| 2000 | 11 | SAT | ALA | AUB | H | 1 | 0-9 | L | -9 | L | -8 |
| 2004 | 9 | SAT | KTKY | GEO | H | 24 | 17-62 | L | -45 | L | -21 |
| 2007 | 2 | SAT | TLN | HOU | H | +14' | 10-34 | L | -24 | L | -9' |

# NCAA FOOTBALL POWER SYSTEM #23

**PRO INFO SPORTS** last look involving how teams do either *before* or *after* facing certain foes, involves how teams do after taking on college foes *N-Z. Section 23* of the **2008 NCAA FOOTBALL POWER SYSTEM e-CYCLOPEDIA** reveals many of these situations, including the one offered below that is perfect since at least 1980 with 18 straight spread wins.

In a very simple but very strong situation, underdogs of more than a TD have rebounded in a big way for 25+ seasons after suffering a loss more than 10 points to Navy.

Play **ON** an underdog of more than 10 points off a SU loss of 11+ points to **Navy**.

SU: 2-16 (-10.7)      **ATS: 18-0 (12.0)**

| YEAR | GM | DAY | TEAM | OPP | ST | LINE | SCORE | SU | MRG | ATS | MRG |
|------|----|-----|------|-----|----|------|-------|----|----|-----|-----|
| 1980 | 11 | SAT | GTCH | GEO | A | +20 | 20-38 | L | -18 | **W** | **+2** |
| 1995 | 3 | SAT | SMU | OKLA | A | +30' | 10-24 | L | -14 | **W** | **+16'** |
| 1996 | 9 | SAT | WAKE | FLST | A | +48' | 7-44 | L | -37 | **W** | **+11'** |
| 1996 | 11 | SAT | TLN | LSU | A | +24 | 17-35 | L | -18 | **W** | **+6** |
| 1997 | 4 | SAT | RUT | BCOL | H | +14' | 21-35 | L | -14 | **W** | **+0'** |
| 1997 | 4 | SAT | SMU | BYU | H | +11 | 16-19 | L | -3 | **W** | **+8** |
| 1997 | 11 | SAT | TEM | WVA | A | +21 | 21-41 | L | -20 | **W** | **+1** |
| 1999 | 3 | SAT | KEST | PIT | A | +33 | 23-30 | L | -7 | **W** | **+26** |
| 1999 | 10 | SAT | RUT | SYR | H | +30' | 24-21 | W | 3 | **W** | **+33'** |
| 2002 | 2 | SAT | SMU | TXT | H | +20 | 14-24 | L | -10 | **W** | **+10** |
| 2003 | 5 | SAT | EMCH | MARY | H | +34 | 13-37 | L | -24 | **W** | **+10** |
| 2003 | 7 | SAT | RICE | FRES | A | +20 | 28-31 | L | -3 | **W** | **+17** |
| 2003 | 10 | SAT | TLN | UAB | A | +13' | 38-24 | W | 14 | **W** | **+27'** |
| 2004 | 2 | SAT | DUKE | CON | A | +15 | 20-22 | L | -2 | **W** | **+13** |
| 2005 | 7 | SAT | RICE | UTEP | H | +18' | 31-38 | L | -7 | **W** | **+11'** |
| 2006 | 10 | SAT | DUKE | BCOL | A | +29 | 7-28 | L | -21 | **W** | **+8** |
| 2006 | 11 | FRI | EMCH | KEST | A | +11' | 6-14 | L | -8 | **W** | **+3'** |
| *2007* | *10* | *THU* | *NTX* | *AKST* | *A* | *+14'* | *27-31* | *L* | *-4* | *W* | *+10'* |

# NCAA FOOTBALL POWER SYSTEM #24

*Section 24* of the **2008 NCAA FOOTBALL e-CYCLOPEDIA** concludes the **PRO INFO SPORTS** examination of regular season **POWER SYSTEMS**. It includes all "miscellaneous" scenarios that didn't fit any of the previous categories. We feature a very strong system from that collection here, as it has gone 20 straight games without a loss just since 1999.

After dropping 2 games as a favorite, teams have been unable to get untracked under the conditions and lines described.

From **Game 5 on,** play **AGAINST** a team (*not* a favorite of more than 5 points *or* underdog of more than 2 points) off 2 favorite SU losses vs. an opponent *not* off an underdog SU loss.

SU: 17-3 (10.4)       **ATS: 19-0-1 (11.9)**

| YEAR | GM | DAY | TEAM | OPP | ST | LINE | SCORE | SU | MRG | ATS | MRG |
|------|----|-----|------|-----|----|----|------|----|----|----|----|
| 1999 | 12 | SAT | PNST | MCST | A | +2 | 28-35 | L | -7 | **L** | **-5** |
| 2000 | 6 | SAT | WYO | SDST | H | -3' | 0-34 | L | -34 | **L** | **-37'** |
| 2000 | 6 | SAT | USC | ORE | H | +1 | 17-28 | L | -11 | **L** | **-10** |
| 2001 | 9 | SAT | UCLA | ORE | H | -1 | 20-21 | L | -1 | **L** | **-2** |
| 2001 | 10 | SAT | UCLA | USC | A | -3' | 0-27 | L | -27 | **L** | **-30'** |
| 2002 | 7 | SAT | UTAH | COST | H | -1 | 20-28 | L | -8 | **L** | **-9** |
| 2002 | 8 | SAT | LTCH | NEV | H | -4' | 50-47 | W | 3 | **L** | **-1'** |
| 2002 | 9 | THU | AIR | COST | H | +1' | 12-31 | L | -19 | **L** | **-17'** |
| 2003 | 7 | SAT | ARK | MIS | A | +1 | 7-19 | L | -12 | **L** | **-11** |
| 2003 | 10 | SAT | NEV | FRES | H | -2' | 10-27 | L | -17 | **L** | **-19'** |
| 2003 | 12 | SAT | UTST | IDA | A | -1 | 13-20 | L | -7 | **L** | **-8** |
| 2004 | 6 | SAT | OHST | IOWA | A | -1 | 7-33 | L | -26 | **L** | **-27** |
| 2004 | 8 | SAT | LLAF | AKST | H | -3 | 27-24 | W | 3 | **P** | **0** |
| 2004 | 9 | SAT | PUR | IOWA | A | -1 | 21-23 | L | -2 | **L** | **-3** |
| 2004 | 9 | SAT | MIZ | KAST | H | -4 | 24-35 | L | -11 | **L** | **-15** |
| 2004 | 11 | SAT | CMCH | BALL | H | -3' | 41-40 | W | 1 | **L** | **-2'** |
| 2005 | 7 | FRI | UAB | SMIS | H | -2' | 28-37 | L | -9 | **L** | **-11'** |
| 2006 | 11 | SAT | MCST | MIN | H | +1' | 18-31 | L | -13 | **L** | **-11'** |
| 2007 | 9 | SAT | SFL | CIN | H | -5 | 33-38 | L | -5 | **L** | **-10** |
| 2007 | 12 | SAT | ORE | ORST | H | 0 | 31-38 | L | -7 | **L** | **-7** |

# NCAA FOOTBALL POWER SYSTEM #25

*Section 25* of the **PRO INFO SPORTS 2008 NCAA FOOTBALL POWER SYSTEM e-CYCLOPEDIA** contains a huge number of **POWER SYSTEMS** for the college post-season. Some apply exclusively to Conference Championship Games, while others apply to Bowl Games only. Still others, like the scenario offered here, apply to both. Such was the case last season with 4 spread wins.

Small favorites and underdogs of 2 TDs or less have been surprisingly strong despite allowing more than 21 points in each of its last 5 games.

Play **ON** a **Conference Championship/Bowl** team (*not* a favorite of 4+ points *or* underdog of more than 14 points) off allowing 22+ points in each of its last 5 games vs. a non-Independent opponent.

SU: 10-3 (7.4)          **ATS: 13-0 (10.3)**

| YEAR | GM | DAY | TEAM | OPP | ST | LINE | SCORE | SU | MRG | ATS | MRG |
|------|----|-----|------|-----|----|------|-------|----|----|----|-----|
| 1999 | 13 | SAT | HAW | ORST | H | +9 | 23-17 | W | 6 | W | +15 |
| 2000 | 12 | THU | WVA | MIS | N | +3' | 49-38 | W | 11 | W | +14' |
| 2000 | 12 | FRI | UCLA | WIS | N | +5' | 20-21 | L | -1 | W | +4' |
| 2000 | 12 | SUN | AIR | FRES | N | +1 | 37-34 | W | 3 | W | +4 |
| 2002 | 13 | TUE | AIR | VTCH | N | +11' | 13-20 | L | -7 | W | +4' |
| 2003 | 13 | WED | BCOL | COST | N | 0 | 35-21 | W | 14 | W | +14 |
| 2004 | 12 | FRI | AZST | PUR | N | +8 | 27-23 | W | 4 | W | +12 |
| 2005 | 12 | FRI | UCLA | NORW | N | -2' | 50-38 | W | 12 | W | +9' |
| 2006 | 13 | THU | OKST | ALA | N | -2 | 34-31 | W | 3 | W | +1 |
| 2007 | 13 | SAT | CMCH | MIAO | N | -3' | 35-10 | W | 25 | W | +21' |
| 2007 | 13 | FRI | FATL | MEM | N | -2' | 44-27 | W | 17 | W | +14' |
| 2007 | 13 | FRI | MCST | BCOL | N | +4' | 21-24 | L | -3 | W | +1' |
| 2007 | 13 | MON | FRES | GTCH | N | +5 | 40-28 | W | 12 | W | +17 |

# THE 2008 NFL & NCAA FOOTBALL

# POWER SYSTEM

## WORKBOOK

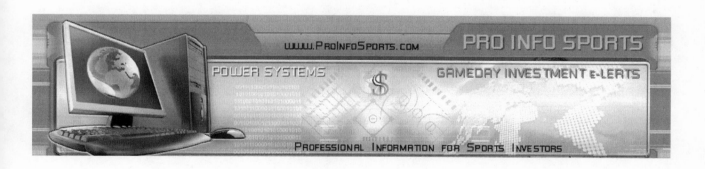

Made in the USA